Hsing-I

By Master James W. McNeil

About Master James W. McNeil

James W. McNeil was born in St Louis, Mo., in 1942 and lived with his brothers and grandparents. He moved to California in 1954 and went to Virgil Jr. High School and Belmont High School, which was close to Los Angeles' famed Chinatown District. McNeil found comfort and enjoyment in spending many hours in Chinatown, although at the time he knew not why. His brother, Frank, belonged to a Haumea Lefiti kung-fu school and often asked him to go. But for almost two years he felt it was not something he needed. In 1966, he finally went to his brother's martial arts school and was amazed at what he saw.

Following is a list of James W. McNeil's martial arts education:

1966-1973: Studied under master Haumea (Tiny) Lefiti. Obtained the highest degree black belt given at that time for splashing hands fighting techniques.

1973-1977: Studied under sifu Ralph Shunn learning shaolin five animals, wing chun, iron hand and received extensive training in all weapons. Obtained the rank of master instructor in June, 1976.

1977-1984: Studied under master Hsu Hong-Chi in Taipai, Taiwan. Received extensive training in the arts of chi kung and hsing-I. Also was taught bone setting, acupressure massage, Taoist sexual techniques and meditation. Obtained fourth-degree black belt in hsing-I in 1983.

1984-1987: Studied under sifu Chin Chen-Yen in Taipai, Taiwan. Trained in the tzu men chuan system (poison fingers) and advanced training in iron hand.

Currently studying with:

• Master Pan Wing-Chow, Taipai, Taiwan, since 1983. Training in Chen style tai chi.

• Master Chiao Chang-Hung, Taipai, Taiwan, since 1983. Receiving advanced training in little nine heaven kung-fu, consisting of fighting, sword and shih shui. Also currently being taught paqua and advanced hsing-I. Further training in Taoist sexual techniques. High levels of chi kung therapy and nei kung meditation is also being be learned.

The author has obtained the following degrees in hypnotherapy:

• Bachelor of Clinical Hypnotherapy degree from the American Institute of Hypnotherapy in 1988.

• Bachelor of Science Hypnotherapy from the American Institute of Hypnotherapy in 1989.

• Doctor of Clinical Hypnotherapy from the American Institute of Hypnotherapy in 1990.

All Rights Reserved.

Printed in the United States of America

ISBN: 0-86568-155-4

Library of Congress Catalog No.: 91-067318

Edited By: Dave Cater

Designed By: Danilo J. Silverio

 **UNIQUE PUBLICATIONS**
4201 Vanowen Place, Burbank, CA 91505

Dedication -

To Master Hsu Hong-Chi

After studying hsing-I for more than 12 years, I am writing this book in honor of my teacher, master Hsu Hong-Chi, and his beloved family. I miss him very much; he not only was a teacher, but a father to many of his students.

Hsu Hong-Chi (1934-1984) was born July 7, 1934 in Taipei, Taiwan, where he lived with his parents and six brothers. At the age of six, Hsu was taken to a Buddhist monk to have his future told. The monk foresaw that Hsu one day would lead a large group of people. Shortly thereafter his father enrolled him in judo and Shaolin kung-fu classes.

After many years of dedicated practice, Hsu realized that to complete his kung-fu he would need to learn the art of hsing-I. This would complete the cycle of yin and yang. Although he worked hard and did well in school, Hsu would have rather practiced kung-fu than study. As his ability and love grew for hsing-I, so did the number of his followers in the International Tang Shou Tao Association. This fulfilled the old monk's prophecy. Hsu lived above his kung-fu school in Taipei with his lovely wife and his four children.

Because of his healing powers, master Hsu was known as, "The man with the magic hands." In Taipei people often came to him for healing, and when he taught in Tokyo, many men, woman and children benefited from his powers. He has also healed many people in the United States.

Master Hsu has appeared in two kung-fu movies and on television in Taiwan, Japan and the United States. He also has been the subject of many newspaper and magazine articles.

When visiting California each year, master Hsu would stay at my home and further my training in the hidden secrets of hsing-I.

Last, but not least, I would like to thank his gracious wife, Mrs. Hsu, for her great kindness and hospitality while I was practicing in Taiwan.

Contents

Preface

I have been studying kung-fu continuously for more than 25 years but I am still learning. There is no end to the knowledge that a person can acquire in this art. Every book that I have read on hsing-I has either left something out or lacked genuine knowledge of hsing-I.

I hope to contribute to a greater understanding of one aspect of Chinese culture which reflects the diversity of influences upon which Chinese civilization was founded. I also hope that by introducing the art of hsing-I to the general public, I can inspire others to take a closer look at a discipline which offers not only physical and health benefits, but psychological ones as well.

In today's stressful world, this surely can be its most important contribution. I wish to thank my teachers, master Hsu Hong-Chi and master Chiao Chang-Hung, for their patience in teaching me hsing-I. They have also shared their vast knowledge in various aspects of Chinese culture. I also wish to thank my senior school brother and dear friend, Carl Kao, and my students, Albert Lam, Gary Doty, Hank Babcock and Jeff Schwartz, for their help in making this book possible. It was through master Hsu Hong-Chi and my hsing-I brother, Carl Kao, that I met my present teachers, master Chiao Chang-Hung (hsiao chiu tien, hsing-I and paqua), and master Pan Wing-Chow (Chen tai chi). Both masters teach the original style, which has been handed down directly from their master and their masters before in China. I truly thank them for their willingness to share their knowledge.

A special thanks to Melinda Goto for her encouragement and many hours of editing.

Names and History

Huang Ti

Huang Ti, the Yellow Emperor and third among China's first five rulers, reigned from 2698-2597 B.C. He is revered today as one of China's most legendary figures.

China's first art of war was initiated by Huang Ti. After numerous battles he brought order to the land. It was from these conflicts, which involved both fierce hand-to-hand fighting and weapons techniques, that engendered our martial arts. He is considered the founder of present-day Chinese civilization

and is also given credit for writing two books that continue to be required reading. His first book, *Nei Ching Su Wen*, is a compilation of the various aspects of Chinese internal medicine and provides the foundation for modern Oriental medicine. A lesser-known text attributed to Huang Ti, *Su Nu Ching*, deals with the use of sexual energy to maintain health and prolong life. It is said that Huang Ti ascended to heaven on the back of a dragon and achieved immortality.

Hsing-I is a Chinese boxing style of Taoist origin and development. It is devoted to the importance of uniting the body and the mind as one. Hsing-I is considered one of the three classical internal arts—tai chi and paqua being its sister arts. As previously stated, the goal of hsing-I is to unite the mind and body. With this unity, the mind can successfully "command" the body and chi. From this comes a devastating martial art. Since it also coordinates, tonifies and regulates the body, good health is a byproduct of hsing-I practice. There is a common misconception that one internal art is superior to another. This is just not true. The three arts are simply different means to the same end.

The research into hsing-I reveals an illustrious and colorful past. There are many stories and anecdotes about the famous masters and their exploits.

Little is known about the creation of hsing-I. The most commonly accepted founder is Yueh Fei (1103-1141), a famous general of the Sung dynasty (960-1276). Yueh Fei hailed from the Honan province and legend has it that he was taught a "divine" art from his Taoist teacher, Chou Ton. Yueh Fei was known

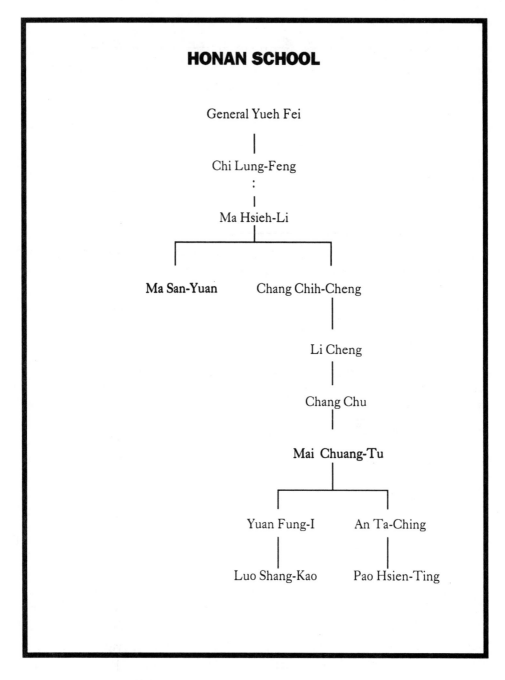

HONAN SCHOOL

General Yueh Fei

Chi Lung-Feng

Ma Hsieh-Li

Ma San-Yuan   Chang Chih-Cheng

Li Cheng

Chang Chu

Mai Chuang-Tu

Yuan Fung-I   An Ta-Ching

Luo Shang-Kao   Pao Hsien-Ting

to be faithful and loyal to his country. It is said that in fighting against foreign tribes, he passed on his hsing-I knowledge to his troops. This gave rise to the saying, "It is easier to fight a mountain than to fight the army of General Yueh Fei."

Because of political jealousy and Yueh Fei's success on the battlefield, he was jailed and later killed at the age of 39. He wrote a manuscript before his death entitled, "Hsing-I," which held the art's entire teachings. It is assumed that a student of Yueh Fei's was entrusted with these teachings.

After Yueh Feh's death, hsing-I was firther popularized by Chi Lung-Feng, who was born at the end of the Ming dynasty. Chi considered his fighting skills as exceptional, but felt there was more to the art. Seeking a teacher with superior skills from whom he could learn, Chi traveled extensively between 1630-1660. He finally located such a man, a Taoist hermit, living at the foot of the Chung Nan Mountains in Shensi province.

The Taoist hermit taught Chi the essence of the art and presented him with an instructional book on the subject. He told Chi that this was the same work written and handed down by General Yueh Fei. Chi studied and practiced enthusiatically day and night until he mastered all the movements. He made such great progress in his hsing-I that no one was able to match his fighting skills. Chi Lung-Feng later taught a great number of students.

Two of Chi Lung-Feng's most famous students, Ma Hsieh-Li and Ts'ao Chi-Wu, later founded their own schools. Ma Hsieh-Li started the Homan school and Ts'ao Chi-Wu founded the Shansi school.

Ma Hsieh-Li was a native of the Honan province. He was brave, clever and quite remarkable in his boxing abilities. Since Ma Hsieh-Li greatly admired Chi's excellent fighting skills, he took a job as a servant at Chi's house. Fearing that Chi might not instruct him, Ma would secretly watch his master practice hsing-I everyday. By practicing everything he saw, Ma learned as much, if not more, than Chi's other disciples.

After serving in the house for almost three years, Ma confessed to Chi Lung-Feng his real purpose for working there and his love for hsing-I. Chi listened and was very pleased with Ma's sincerity. He asked Ma to demonstrate what he had learned through his observations and was impressed. Chi asked Ma to become a student and eventually taught Ma the fighting skills of hsing-I.

Many years later, Ma Hsieh-Li returned to his native province and began the Honan branch of hsing-I. Two of his best students were Ma San-Yuan and Chang Chih-Cheng.

Ma San-Yuan was a native of Nan-Yang, Honan province, and known for his love of fighting. Stories abound that he killed over 40 men in challenge matches. Ma San-Yuan went crazy later in life and never taught students. Chang Chih-Cheng was a good friend and school brother of Ma San-Yuan's. However, he was very different from Ma San-Yuan. Chang didn't fight as often but was highly skilled in the art of hsing-I. He was very selective in choosing his students, the best of which was his nephew, Li Cheng. Under the guidance of his uncle, Li Cheng became proficient in hsing-I. He worked as a bodyguard for supply convoys and could often be found practicing the chicken, his favorite form. In his free time, he would often use the chicken step to chase the horses or mules. Li taught many students in the Honan province, the best being Chang Chu.

A close friend of Li Cheng, Chang Chu was in the restaurant business. Li taught Chang only the choice cuts of the hsing-I system. Chang learned well and passed on his knowledge to his son and his nephew, Mai Chuang-Tu.

The Shansi System

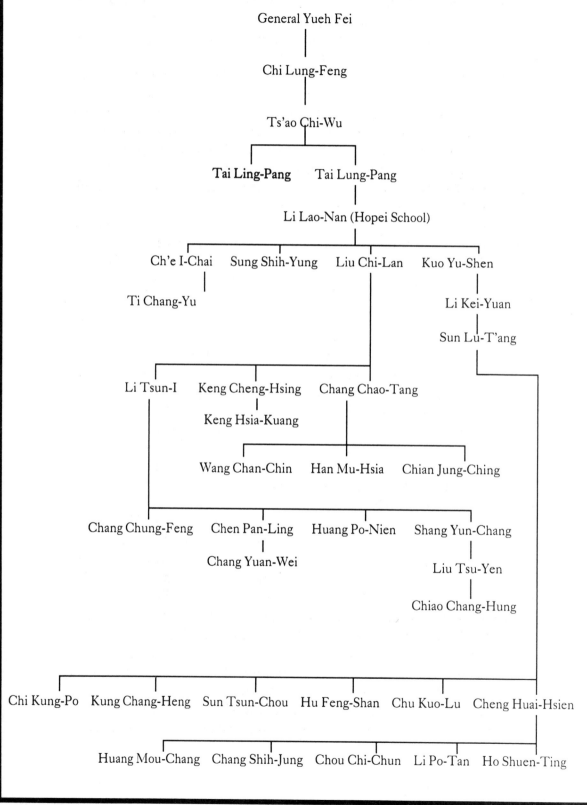

General Yueh Fei

Chi Lung-Feng

Ts'ao Chi-Wu

Tai Ling-Pang   Tai Lung-Pang

Li Lao-Nan (Hopei School)

Ch'e I-Chai   Sung Shih-Yung   Liu Chi-Lan   Kuo Yu-Shen

Ti Chang-Yu

Li Kei-Yuan

Sun Lu-T'ang

Li Tsun-I   Keng Cheng-Hsing   Chang Chao-Tang

Keng Hsia-Kuang

Wang Chan-Chin   Han Mu-Hsia   Chian Jung-Ching

Chang Chung-Feng   Chen Pan-Ling   Huang Po-Nien   Shang Yun-Chang

Chang Yuan-Wei

Liu Tsu-Yen

Chiao Chang-Hung

Chi Kung-Po   Kung Chang-Heng   Sun Tsun-Chou   Hu Feng-Shan   Chu Kuo-Lu   Cheng Huai-Hsien

Huang Mou-Chang   Chang Shih-Jung   Chou Chi-Chun   Li Po-Tan   Ho Shuen-Ting

Chang Chu's son mastered hsing-I by the time he was 15, but died at an early age. After his son's death, Mai Chuang-Tu was Chang's only disciple.

Mai Chuang-Tu practiced hard everyday and came to regard the chicken as his favorite animal form. Mai lived two miles from town and would cover the distance using the chicken step. This provided a great deal of humor for the townspeople. Mai was known for his gentleness, but when he fought he became a man of great strength and technique.

One of Mai's top students was a Muslim named An Ta-Ching, who would tell people that hsing-I was the easiest style to learn but the hardest to master. An Ta-Ching believed hsing-I was often misunderstood because it appeared too easy and natural. His best student was Pao Hsien-Ting, who also was of the Muslim faith and among the most intelligent martial artists of the time. He was proficient in all styles and had been instructed by more than ten teachers. A highly skilled fighter, Pao sought additional knowledge by studying with An Ta-Ching. Within a few years he became the master's top disciple. After boxing was prohibited in 1900 by the Ching dynasty, An Ta-Ching joined the army and helped repel the Communists. Once the Communist threat was over, An Ta-Ching returned to teaching and created his own system. In 1921, he founded the Chi Chien Martial Arts Society. He died in 1947 at the age of 87.

Ts'ao Chi-Wu, a native of Shanghai, learned hsing-I directly from Chi Lung-Feng. Ts'ao practiced his hsing-I diligently everyday and became known for his great ability. Later in life, Ts'ao Chi-Wu was named the commanding general of Shansi province. Because of his military genius, the troops under his command won a great many battles over the Muslim tribes. After retiring from the army, Ts'ao devoted himself to perfecting his hsing-I. He taught many students but the brothers Tai were the most well-known.

Tai Lung-Pang and Tai Ling-Pang were natives of the Che Hsien of Shansi province. They practiced hard and quickly learned. They were Ts'ao's best students. Tai Ling-Pang, however, was not as famous as his brother who had many students, one of whom was Li Lao-Nan.

After meeting the Tai brothers and seeing their skills, Li asked if he could study with them. He started learning hsing-I at the relatively late age of 37. Li practiced hard for ten years, during which Tai Lung-Pang taught him everything he knew. Because of his hsing-I knowledge, Li was undefeated in boxing. It was said he could defeat opponents from a great distance and also jump eight feet into the air at any given moment. Some of Li's skills were so incredible that people referred to his style as "divine boxing." Thanks to his prowess, hsing-I became widespread in many provinces of China. Li had a great number of students and among them were Ch'e I-Chai, Kuo Yun-Shen and Shung Shih-Yung. All became well-known for their hsing-I abilities. Li Nao Nan lived to be more than 80. Ch'e I-Chai (1831-1912), a native of the Shansi province, was warm-hearted, even-tempered, and mutually respected.

He practiced hsing-I for many years and became Li Lao-Nan's best student. Ch'e also was the only person to defeat Kuo Yun-Shen (other than paqua master Tung Hai-Chuan). Ch'e lived to be 81.

Shung Shih-Yung, a native of Shansi province, was also a student of Li Lao-Nan's and a schoolmate of Kuo Yun-Shen. Shung was noted for his agility and flexibility. With only a slap of his hand he could throw a challenger several feet. In later years he devoted himself to a Buddhist Temple and no longer talked of fighting. He passed on his knowledge to only one student, Kuo Yun-Shen. He was a native of Shen Hsien, around the same area where Li Lao-Nan was born. Kuo possessed great hsing-I ability and developed a skill equal to that of Li Lao-Nan's. He became well-known for his half-step and crushing style and usually defeated his enemy with only one punch. This led to his style becoming known as the "divine crushing hand."

One day, Kuo accepted a challenge fight in Hopei. The fight began and with only one punch Kuo killed his opponent. As a result, he was imprisoned for three years. While in prison he practiced hard and after his release was stronger and quicker than before. People would describe him as, "half-step, wood punch, conquers the whole world." Kuo believed that Taoist meditation was similar to hsing-I, in that both promoted total emptiness. He said when you fight someone, look to see how strong, soft or muscular he is and discover his weak points. Then, if you must fight, end it as quickly as you can. Sadly, when he died at 70, he took with him many of his secrets.

Li Kuei-Yuan was a native of Lai-Chui Hsien, Hopei province. He was highly skilled in the art of Shaolin kung-fu. Later in life, he learned hsing-I from Kuo Yu-Shen. After studying hard for several years, he became Kuo's best student. Li's number-one student was Sun Lu-T'ang.

Sun Lu-T'ang (1859-1933) was a native of Hobei province and was very famous for his martial art skills. It is said he had mastered all three internal styles. Sun had many fights but was never defeated. Sun's hsing-I teachers were Li Kuei-Yuan and Kuo Yun-Shen, but most of his hsing-I knowledge came from Kuo Yun-Shen. Sun learned his paqua from Cheng Ting-Hua. He taught many students and some of his best were: Chi Kung-Po, Kung Chang-Heng, Sun Ysun-Chou, Hu Feng-Shan, Chun Luo-Lu and Cheng Hua-Hsien. Sun wrote two books on hsing-I and another on tai chi. He also authored a book on paqua and the paqua sword. He died Dec. 26, 1933 at 73.

Cheng Huai-Hsien was born in 1896. He was experienced in paqua, hsing-I, tai chi, chin na and push hands. Cheng studied under Sun Lu-T'ang for many years. When he was 12, Cheng learned northern style kung-fu and a year later had mastered approximately 20 movements of the flying fork style system. His desire to further study the flying fork system later in life led him to a famous teacher, Li Yuh-Ching. Cheng studied with Li for eight years and learned an additional 30 movements of the flying fork style. After traveling extensively, Cheng found a teacher who taught him 20 more movements. By putting together the different movements, Cheng created his own system, which consisted of 90 techniques. Cheng felt his flying fork system was too difficult to master and he never passed his knowledge onto any students. However, he had many hsing-I students. One of his best was Ho Shuen-Ting.

When he was 24 years of age, Cheng began studying hsing-I, paqua and tai chi from Sun Lu-T'ang. After practicing for eight years, Sun introduced Cheng to Le Fong-Tzeng who taught him the sword. Cheng ultimately taught almost 1,000 students. He never refused a student nor accepted money. He taught whatever the student wanted to learn and he never hid anything. Cheng died Oct. 31, 1981, at the age of 84. Although he had two sons and a daughter, they never studied kung-fu.

Chen Chi-Lin was born in Han Tsou City, China, in 1903. At an early age Chen began studying Shaolin kung-fu. From 1920-1930, Chen mastered hsing-I from one of Sun Lu-T'ang's senior students. He also mastered the original five animal tai chi and meditation. Today, Master Chen lives in Los Angeles, Ca and is 87 years old. James W. McNeil, the author of this book, was one of master Chen's many students. Master Chen's senior student is Dr. C.H. Poon, who also teaches in the Los Angeles area.

Ho Shuen-Ting was born in Shiang Tan, China, and learned hsing-I and paqua while in the military. In 1940, he was transferred to the Szechwan province and met his future teacher, Cheng Huai-Hsien. It was during the Communist takeover in 1949 that Ho escaped to Taiwan. Master Ho is a retired Air Force General and the current martial arts professor at the Taiwan University. He also teaches in Texas and at the author's school in Southern California.

Liu Chi-Lan was a native of Shen Hsien, Hopei province, and spent many years under the guidance of Li Lao Nan. Although not as well-known as his classmates, Liu nevertheless was very good. He devoted his life to spreading his knowledge of hsing-I. He had many famous disciples, Li Tsun-I being the foremost. Liu felt that for hsing-I to conform with Taoist principles, "Your mind must be mindless and your body bodiless."

Li Tsun-I (1850-1925), also known as "Knife Li," was a native of Hopei province. He became the best and most famous disciple of Liu Chi-Lan's. Li's fame spread throughout China through his numerous disciples and by his exploits as a convoy guard. Chang Chung-Feng, Chen Pan-Ling, Huang Po-Nien and Shung Shih-Yung were Li's best students.

Chen Pan-Ling (1900-1967) graduated from Peking University, with a degree in civil engineering. He devoted his life to the Chinese government, where he held several important positions, including that of vice president of the Chung Kuo Shu Academy. Later, he was head of a government committee under the Department of Education and Military Training. This committee compiled more than 50 standardized martial arts texts and also collected illustrations of at least 40 variations of styles. However, these materials were lost when the Communists took over Mainland China. It was during this time that master Chen departed for Taiwan.

After working on their farm in China, Chen and his four brothers would study Shaolin kung-fu from their father. Master Chen became an expert in tai chi, Shaolin, hsing-I, paqua and several

types of weapons. Chen and master Chiao Chang Hung later founded the Martial Arts Society of the Republic of China. Chang Yuan-Wei became master Chen's best student.

Chang Yuan-Wei was born in Cheking, China. Through his early years he was sickly and weak. Fortunately, he met his teacher, master Chin Pan-Ling, who taught him hsing-I, paqua and tai chi. For several decades, Chang has practiced the arts daily, regretting only that he was not as good as his teacher. Nonetheless, he knew the benefits he received from practice, because now, at more than 70 years of age, he can climb a mountain as if he were walking down a city street. He credits daily practice of his art for this miraculous change in health. Chang was a colonel in the Chinese Air Force in the Republic of China for 30 years before he retired to Taiwan. He has also studied aeronautical engineering in both China and the United States. Chang now resides and teaches in Montgomery, Ala. The author and master Chang enjoy a very strong friendship.

Huang Po-Nien was born in China and was a student of Li Tsing-I's. Huang taught the soldiers of the military to incorporate hsing-I with the military sword and the bayonet. He later authored a book on the use of the military bayonet

and sword in combination with hsing-I.

Chang Chung-Feng was from Tientsin, China, and fled to Taiwan with the nationalists in 1948. He taught many people in Taiwan, one of his students being Hung I-Hsuang.

Hung I-Hsuang was born in Taiwan and studied Shaolin kung-fu until he was introduced to Chang Chun-Feng in 1948 by master Chiao Chang-Hung. He was large for a Chinese and had a reputation of being a highly skilled fighter. Today, he spends his time overseeing his son's teaching in Taipei, Taiwan, as well as working as a traditional doctor. One of Hung I-Hsuang's best students was Hsu Hong-Chi.

Hsu Hong-Chi was the author's teacher from 1977 until his death in 1984. A brief history on Hsu Hong-Chi can be found on the dedication page of this book. In Taiwan his best students were Hsu Chang-Wang, his son, and Carl Kao. According to Hsu Hong-Chi, a student of hsing-I should be wise but ignorant, because a wise man does not show his skill unless he has to. One should keep everything to himself. In a real fight, one should feel emptiness and act like no one is there. When attacking, the hands and body should move together. The hands should be alive and the legs light. If every step and strike are coordinated, one will not lose the upper hand to the opponent.

Hsu Chang-Wang is a native of Taipei, Taiwan. He has studied hsing-I with his father for most of his life. Hsu Chang-Wang has taken over the leadership of the International Tang Shou Tao Association in Taiwan since his father's death and currently teaches a large number of students in Taipei. He also remains undefeated in many full-contact tournaments.

Carl Kao was born in Taipei, Taiwan. He started studying hsing-I with master Hsu Hong-Chi at a young age. By the time he was 17 Carl had became the number-one student of master Hsu. He has also studied hsing-I, paqua and little nine heaven kung-fu from master Chiao Chang-Hung. He also has learned Chen tai chi from master Pan Wing-

Chow. Currently living in Florida, Carl teaches government officials in Malaysia, Japan, Hong Kong and Singapore. He also was a teacher at the Chinese Culture College for seven years.

Shang Yun-Chang (1863-1938) was born in Shantung, China, and was one of Li Ts'un-I's best students. He was small but extremely powerful. Shang was very outspoken and would fight anyone. An illiterate, he used a "hands-on" approach to show techniques. As a result, Shang lost many students. Some students died from injuries received in sparring with Shang. Liu Tsu-Yen was one of Shang's best students.

Liu Tsu-Yen was among a handful of students who stayed with Shang Yun-Chang. Liu's teaching methods were very similar to his master's. After many years, Liu went to Shen Yang City, China, and become the chief martial arts instructor for the North Eastern military division. Liu was a true master of hsing-I and tai chi. His best and most famous student was Chiao Chang-Hung.

Chiao Chang-Hung, whose hometown is located in the northeastern region of China, is now 75 years old. Master Chiao encountered an extraordinary master in the San Ching Taoist Temple, located at the top of the Wu Lu Shan mountain in China. Chiao was asked by the high priest to be his disciple. Upon moving into the temple, Chiao began to learn the ancient art of kung-fu called hsiao chiu tien or little nine heaven. This style consists of boxing, swordsmanship and shih shui kung-fu. He was taught hsing-I and tai chi from his father's friend, Liu Tsu-Yen in Shen Yang City, China. Later, he learned Ma-Wei-Chi style paqua from Yang Ju-Lin, who was the top apprentice of the paqua palm master Ma Wei-Chi. Master Chiao can also claim mastery in hsing-I, paqua, tai chi and little nine heaven. Master Chiao is the author's current teacher.

Basic Exercises

The saying, "Hurting one's fists while punching others and hurting one's feet while kicking others," warns us that even though there are many varieties of attack, we may not always subdue our enemy. Strength applied in self-defense must be sufficient to hurt the opponent. There are no absolute methods that guarantee the weak overcoming the strong. Therefore, we must have some basic training to guarantee swifter, surer and better methods of self-defense.

Another reason behind basic exercises is body conditioning. This improves one's health and ultimately lengthens one's life span. It is essential to keep the body in top condition to achieve the best results from any technique. Flexibility is important because the more flexible you are, the more fluid and free your movements will be. The tighter the tendon, the shorter the lifespan will be, which is why you should always combine external and internal exercises. Listed below are a few examples:

Breathing

Because all other functions depend on breathing, it is considered the most important function of the body. We all can exist for some time without eating and a shorter time without water, but without air, our existence is measured in minutes. It is the first thing given to us and the last thing taken away, yet many take breathing for granted.

We go to various health clubs to tone our external bodies so that we may look good, but we seldom think about toning our inner organs by doing proper breathing exercises. This promises to keep the body healthy and free of disease. Illustrated are the three kinds of breathing

1. Upper breathing, in which only one-third of our lungs is used.

2. Middle breathing, in which only two-thirds of our lungs are used.

3. Complete breathing, in which the total lung capacity is used. We were all meant to breathe in this way, just as we did when we were infants. Only with complete breathing can all stagnant air be removed from the bottom of our lungs and replaced with fresh air. Using this technique will keep one healthy and free of disease.

The first exercise shows how to properly breathe using the entire lung. This type of breathing is important in hsing-I, as well as in the other internal systems. First stand up, flatten your tongue against the roof of your mouth and gently close your mouth. Inhale through your nose to the lower part of your stomach, which the Chinese call the tan tien. The tan tien is located three inches below your navel. Inhale and the stomach expands, exhale and it contracts. By putting your hand on your stomach you will be reminded that you should always breathe this way.

This is the proper breathing method and should be practiced every day. Proper breathing can be practiced when one is sitting or walking, and especially while practicing hsing-I. Practice this breathing method until it becomes habit. Breathing this way means the entire lung capacity is being used. Never inhale and exhale through your mouth, and always keep your mouth closed and breathe through your nose. Also, do not expand your chest when inhaling. Keep the chest relaxed and breathe abdominally.

Flapping Exercise

Stand with your feet approximately a shoulder-width apart and raise your hands straight out at level shoulders.

1. Flap your hands inward toward your stomach then outward in front of you in a whipping motion at about chest level.

2. Flap them to the side, as far as you can, in a relaxed manner. Raise your arms again to shoulder level.

3. Flap them down as far as you can, then over your head. This is done in a relaxed manner.

Beginners should practice up to 60 times a day.
Advanced should practice up to 200 times a day.

Many people who suffer from digestive problems such as irregularity will greatly benefit from doing this exercise.

Push-Ups

1. Get on the floor face down and stretch out your body. Support your body with your fists and toes. Begin the exercise by straightening your arms, thereby raising your body, then bend your arms to lower your body to the floor. Repeat this sequence the required number of times.

2. Get on the floor face down and stretch out your body. Support your body with your fingertips and toes. Don't bend your fingertips; keep them straight. Begin the exercise by straightening your arms, thereby raising your body, then bend your arms to lower your body to the floor.

Beginners should practice 10-to-15 times.

This exercise must be done slowly and with strength. Breathe out when going down and breathe in when coming up. The body must be straight throughout the exercise, which should be done without bending the waist or knees. The hands should be about a shoulder-width apart.

Dragon Push-Ups

Fists should be a shoulder-width apart, with the feet spread wider than the shoulders and the buttocks higher than the head. Lower the head so it is parallel to the ground. Arch your body with your head up and the eyes staring upward. Lower your head back toward the ground, then go back to the beginning position.

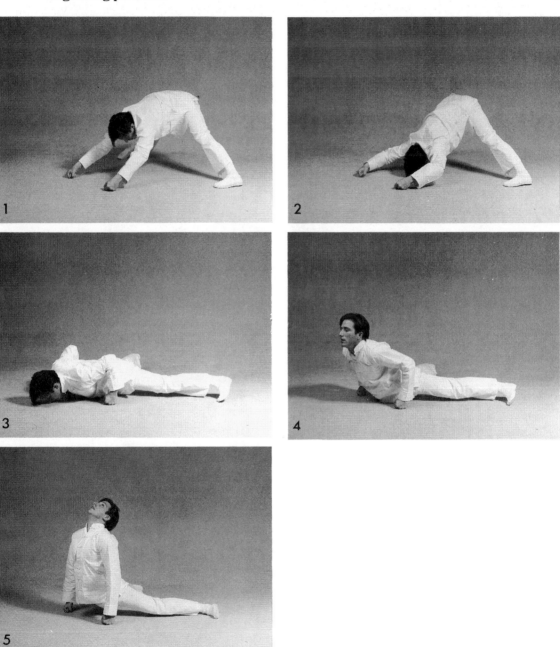

Repeat this exercise as many times as possible.

Throwing the Sand Bags (Two-person exercise)

The sand bag is a small canvas bag filled with a mixture of fine sand, sawdust or green peas and weighing approximately two pounds. One should start with a two-pound bag and slowly increase the bag's weight by two- or three-pound increments. Beginning throwers should start at least nine or ten feet apart and advanced students approximately 20-to-25 feet apart.

Method

Students should grasp and throw the bag as if playing catch. Remember to relax the muscles and breath naturally. Alternate the left and right hands for grasping and throwing. Throwing the sand bag can sharpen reaction time, as well as develop grasping accuracy and speed. It can also help develop agility and strength.

Sit-Ups

First Position

Stretch your body on the floor, face upward and hands behind your head. Have someone sit on your lower legs. Raise and lower your body, touching your elbows to your knees. Then continue to the next position.

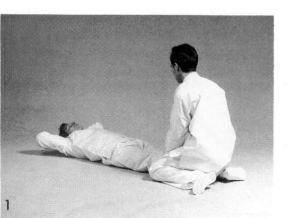 

Second Position

Turn over and have someone sit on the back of your lower legs. Begin by arching and raising your head as much as possible. Your eyes are staring at the sky.

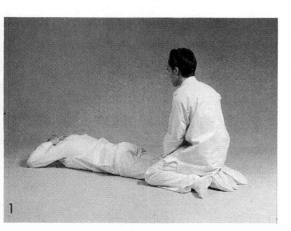 

Third Position

Turn on your right side and have someone sit on your lower legs. With your hands behind your head, raise your body and try to touch your elbow to your hip.

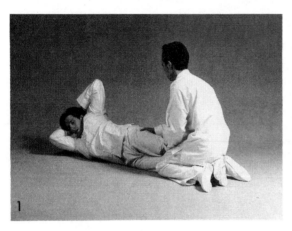

Fourth Position

Turn over on your left side and have someone sit on your lower legs. With your hands behind your head, raise your body and try to touch your elbow to your hip.

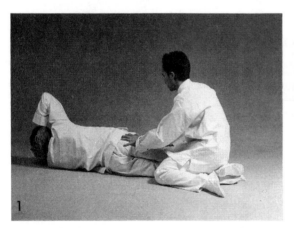

Note:
Beginners should practice using sets consisting of 10-to-15 sit-ups per position. Advanced students should practice using sets consisting of 50 sit-ups per position.

This exercise must be done slowly and with strength. The person sitting on your legs should not put too much weight on your legs. This exercise is designed to equally strengthen all sides of your body.

The Internal Aspect

The internal aspect of martial arts is a subject discussed by everyone who practices kung-fu, but is known and actually employed by only a few. It is the power you cannot see because it comes from within. Developing your chi requires daily practice. The subtle changes that occur take place gradually. Don't expect to see the change overnight; it takes a great deal of time and patience to cultivate.

"Qi" (chi) is the Chinese term that refers to the vital force which permeates the body and gives us life. "Qigong" (chi kung) refers to "ability" or "techniques" to cultivate chi and freely circulate it through the body for good health and long life. "Tao" refers to the "way" or "path" that nourishes life. The ancient Taoists developed extraordinary abilities through the practice and perfection of methods that cultivate chi. They could nourish their existence and cultivate a healthy, energetic lifespan, with some living to be from 100-to-150 years of age.

By practicing every day you will strengthen the internal organs and reduce stress on your nervous system. Daily practice also will greatly improve your overall health. The following exercises constitute some of the best known to martial artists. Remember to practice these exercises daily. With practice, your hsing-I will improve and good health will be the result.

Shaolin Three Exercises

Exercise 1

Position your body (1). Rest your palms flat on the ground and under your lower back. Relax and breath naturally through your nose. Inhale deeply. Let your lower belly expand as you inhale and remain fully expanded as you hold your breath. Raise your hips (2). Hold the position as long as you can. Exhale slowly as you return to the ground.

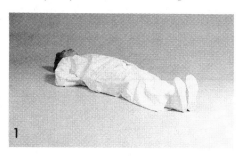 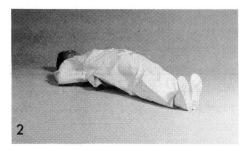

Exercise 2

Position yourself (1). Inhale deeply, expanding your abdomen. Hold your breath and make sure the back of your hands are against the kidneys. Raise your hips off the ground(2). Hold your breath as long as you can. Exhale slowly as you return to the starting position.

Exercise 3

Position yourself(1). Hold your breath and raise your legs and torso(2). Hold your breath as long as you can. Return to the starting position. This completes one cycle. You should do each cycle three-to-five times.

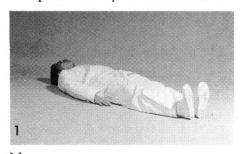 

Note:

Do not underestimate this exercise. It is very beneficial for building lower abdominal strength. You should begin to feel the results within several weeks.

Tiger Playing with the Ball

Begin this exercise with your left hand and forearm parallel to the ground in front of you and at the upper chest level. The shoulders are relaxed. The right hand and arm are parallel to the navel (1). Inhale through the nose as you twist to the right (2). Overturn your hands and exhale as you twist slowly to the left (3). It is best if the exhalation lasts the duration of the twist. Repeat this exercise at least 12 times.

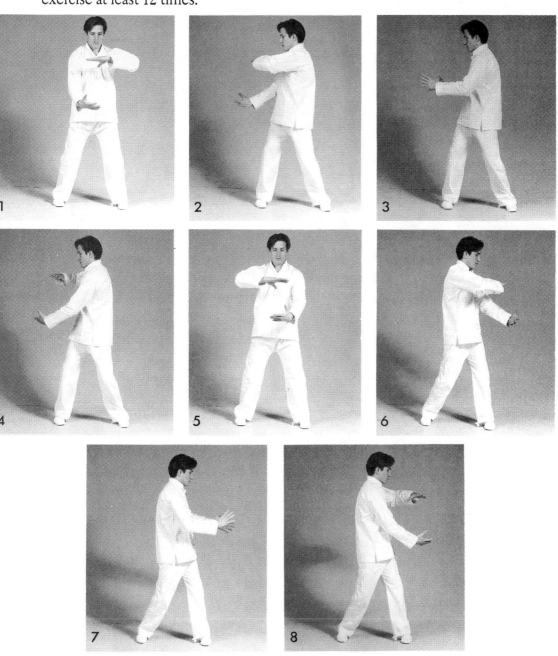

Reaching for the Heaven and Earth

Begin this exercise by opening your legs until they are about a shoulder-width apart. The hands are at the solar plexus level (1). While inhaling, the left palm moves downward and to the rear and the right palm moves upward (2). Turn the upper torso slightly to the left. The eyes watch the right heel. Keep this position as long as you can hold your breath. The fingertips of both hands point to the rear. Now begin to relax as you exhale. Repeat this exercise in the opposite direction.

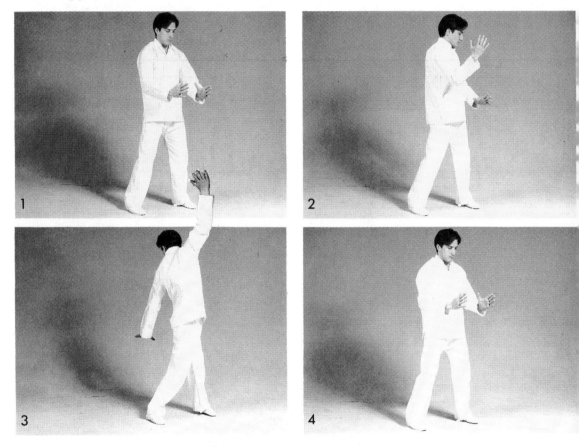

Note: This exercise is good for stretching the abdominal muscles and chest. It improves circulation of blood and chi, increases lung capacity, clears the throat and helps calm your mind.

Standing Meditation

When standing in this position for about 45 minutes, with both arms forming a circle and your fingertips almost touching, you will notice your arms and back begin to feel sore and hot. The more you practice, the sooner the soreness will leave and you will feel warmth or tingling. Both feet should be rooted with your weight equally distributed. To connect the yin and yang meridians, the tongue should touch the roof. The mind should be relaxed and your breathing deep and natural. Once you have developed basic chi flowing, one should begin to concentrate on directing chi from one arm to the other. The chi flows out as you exhale and exchanges at the fingertips into the other arm as you inhale. This will cause the chi to flow from one hand to the other and back again into your body, thus forming a circle of chi. If practiced diligently, this exercise will improve your general health and strength and gradually develop internal chi power.

Sitting Meditation (Taoist Meditation)

Before starting Taoist meditation, you should first find a comfortable and quiet place where you will not be disturbed. Sit with your legs crossed on a firm thick pad, either on the floor or in a chair. All your attention should be focused on the lower tan tien. Your tongue should be placed firmly against the roof of

 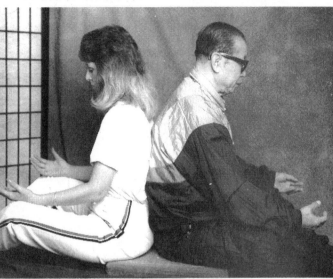

your mouth while doing natural lower abdomen breathing. Sit still and do nothing. Try to empty the mind of all conceptual thoughts. Sitting still and doing nothing is the only way to give your mind a complete rest. One hour of deep meditation is equivalent to eight hours of sleep. Taoist meditation can also be practiced back to back. However, this should be practiced by advanced students only. In this type of meditation, two people, preferably male and female, practice directing their chi and energy to and thru each other's body. This training should be taught by a qualified instructor. After practicing this method of meditation for approximately three months, you should begin to circulate your energy around the body. This is called the microcosmic orbit. Inhale and the energy will go up the back of your body; exhale and the energy will go down the front of your body. This is very beneficial for your health, as well as for anyone who suffers from high blood pressure, indigestion, premature ejaculation, hypertension, anxiety, stress and an imbalance in vital functions. There is nothing mysterious or magical about meditation. One should just completely relax and let whatever happens happen. Be patient—all good things comes to those who wait.

The Eight Fundamentals of Hsing-I

If you wish to master the art of hsing-I, you must first learn and follow the eight fundamentals. These pictures show both the correct and incorrect ways.

The Three Press-Ups: Head, Tongue and Palms

The Head: The head is the headquarters of the body. When the head lifts, the chi can easily travel along the back of the body to the top of the head. This is very beneficial to one's health.

The Tongue: When pressed upward against the palate, the tongue will help the chi to move downward to the tan tien. The tongue works as a switch with saliva as the conductor. This keeps the mouth in a condition which helps control thirst.

The Palm: When pressed outward in the proper position, the palm will help the chi extend to each part of the body. This also helps to strengthen the arms.

The Three Suppresses: Shoulder, Hands and Teeth

Shoulder: The shoulders suppress, so that the front of the chest will feel empty and strength will flow down to the elbows.

Hands: The hands and feet work as one unit. Suppress the hands with the upper arms, but be relaxed. The feet, waist and back are to be closely linked.

Teeth: The teeth and chin suppress downward, so that the ligaments and bones feel tight.

The Three Rounds: Back, Chest and Hands

Back: The back is slightly rounded, so that one is relaxed and ready.

Chest: The chest is rounded to give full strength when power is needed and to permit smooth, relaxed breathing.

Hands: The hands will be rounded and relaxed so chi can be felt.

The Three Sensitives: Eyes, Heart and Hands

Eyes: The eyes are sensitive windows and can give away one's feelings. When facing an opponent you should be confident and fierce.

Heart: The heart controls the mind, so the quality of your heart can either help or destroy you. One should be alert and clever and quickly respond. You must maintain a fierce attitude in life-and-death situations.

Hands: The hands are sensitive so they will quickly move and respond to each situation. The hands will eventually become like the eyes.

The Three Holdings: Tan Tien, Breath and Arms

Tan Tien: The tan tien is to be filled with chi; this is the reservoir of life energy.
Breath: Holding the breath will bring many health benefits.
Arms: Holding the arms in the proper way will build strength and endurance.

The Three Sinkings: Chi, Shoulders and Elbows

Chi: The sinking of chi to the tan tien helps the body become strong and transcend physical limitations. It also helps you overcome many illnesses.
Shoulders: The sinking of the shoulders can bring about both relaxation and power. This is done in conjunction with the suppressing of the shoulders.
Elbows: The sinking of the elbows will provide protection to the ribs.

The Three Curves: Elbows, Wrists and Knees

Elbows: The elbows curve and will be full of energy. Proper angle allows full chi flow.
Wrists: The wrists curve and will allow chi flow.
Knees: The knees curve and the cycle of power is fulfilled.

In all the curves, one should be stretched and extended, but one should also have the flexibility to recoil without tension.

The Three Straightenings: Neck, Spine and Knees

Neck: With the neck straightened, the head is upright and energy will flow to the top of the head.
Spine: With the spine straightened, chi will flow throughout the body.
Knees: With the knees straightened and firmly rooted, one will surely feel the power of chi. This straightness refers to reaching outward with the advanced leg.

The Nine Essences

Body: Should never be leaning forward, backward, to the left or right. But should be straight.

Shoulder: Should be downward. Let your shoulders move together. It is through the shoulders that the strength in the body is transferred to your hands.

Arms: The left arm is stretched forward. The right arm is held close to your ribs. It should be bent but not contracted, stretched but not stiff. Too contracted, it can never reach far. Too straight, it cannot be powerful.

Hands: The right hand is held at the tan tien. The left hand is held at chest level. The latter is relaxed, the former should have strength. Both hands are held palms down. Strength in each hand should be even.

Fingers: Each are separated and shaped as hooks. The index finger and thumb form a crescent. The fingers are held with strength, but are not forced.

Legs: The left leg is to the front, right leg held behind. Be straight but not stiff. Be bowed slightly, yet straight overall. This is being straight yet bowed like a chicken.

Feet: All toes pointing forward, never to the sides. Right back foot at a 45-degree sideward stance. Distance is up to the individual. Toes should be firm.

Tongue: Chi will be weak if the tongue is not rolled. It sinks to the tan tien when the eyes are lowered. The muscles of the face are like iron and the inner organs are strengthened.

Hips: Tilted a little bit forward, so chi can be moved to the limbs. Otherwise it will be scattered throughout the body.

Combination of Six

Hsing-I is an extremely powerful, yet practical self-defense fighting style. All the power is generated from the tan tien, the center of the body's balance and energy. The rule of the six styles was developed to help one understand how the body acts.

The Six Styles of the Body

1. Chicken legs
2. Dragon body
3. Eagle claws
4. Bear shoulders
5. Tiger embrace
6. Thunder and roaring

No matter how it is changed, a style cannot pull away from its origins. In hsing-I, we use light and powerfully mobile chicken legs and the indomitable strength of the dragon body. This is combined with the engulfing, crushing force of bear shoulders and the gripping, rending slash of the eagle claws. The body's movements should be like a monkey; neither leaning forward nor backward, but must always be centered to facilitate for quick and balanced movement. The expulsion of breath is as the sound of thunder from within as the chi fills the body and begs release.

When viewed from the front, the body should look as if it were facing to the side. From the side, it should seem to face the front. This is an extremely subtle compromise in body placement and can only be learned from a competent teacher.

The front leg should be light, the back leg solid. The legs should be neither straight nor bent. If kept too straight or bent too much, you will be unstable. The force of the hand should be in the wrist and its power should be transmitted to the fingers. The shoulders should drop. If the shoulders are too high they become stiff and cannot move quickly into a full and devastating attack. The six styles are used in combination with the seven stars.

Seven Stars

A strike follows a chain of movements. It begins with the foot and follows through to every joint and finally ends at the hand. This creates the theory of the seven stars of hsing-I. The seven stars are: the head, shoulder, elbow, hand, hip, knee and foot. They can be used either as a single striking entity or in combination. They are the weapons of the human body that can attack with great power. With these rules come the means by which one can successfully deliver an attack.

To strike: To use all of one's inner power to move the hands and legs together. Fists as cannons, body as a dragon, alive and deadly. Move as if you have flames running all over your body in the face of an attacker.

Head hit: The body moves as one. The feet are aligned under the body along the centerline.

Shoulder hit: One is yin (back), one is yang (front) and the hands are hidden. The front hand is aligned with the nose to appear hidden from the front. The rear hand centers on the chest and seems concealed from the side. Use either right or left hand depending on the situation.

Hand hit: Moving from your chest, the hands are like a powerful tiger catching a delicate lamb. The strength in your hands should instantly be interchangeable. Elbows are to be lowered to protect the body and explode with power.

Hip hit: Yin or yang, left or right; it depends on the situation. Be natural while moving the feet and be quick as lightning while attacking.

Knee hit: Knee strikes against any vital point can be fatal. The hands are held up in front to balance the body.

Foot hit: Steps are firm. The strength comes from one foot rooted to the ground. Never fake a leg attack. Kick only with a full-power shot to a vital spot.

Six Harmonies

External Body

Shoulder   *Yang*   The shoulder matches the opposite hip.

Hips   *Yin*   The twisting of the waist creates greater power when the waist is quickly released.

Elbow   *Yang*   The elbows and knees move as one to produce more power.

Knee   *Yin*   Too lose power when the elbows extend past the knee.

Hand   *Yang*   The hands and feet move together for greater speed and power.

Feet   *Yin*   Use the feet in combination with the hands.

By mastering the six harmonies and using them in conjunction, one will have greater internal strength and power.

Internal

Heart matches the mind:
The heart and mind are the origin of all action. If you want to kill, the heart must turn cold.

Mind matches the chi:
Chi is directed anywhere within the body by the concentration of the mind.

Chi matches strength:
Matching chi and strength means that the muscles and bones join to produce a tremendous power called chi kung.

During regular practice, one should act as if facing a top opponent. However, in a real fight, one cultivates emptiness of mind through meditation and reacts like an echo. When attacking, step forward, constantly oriented to the center gate. The hand and body move together. The hand should be alive and flexible, the leg light and ready to move. One should move left, right or back using one's nose as the cross hairs. Attacking is attacking and retreating is retreating. One can efficiently block or strike while retreating or advancing. Every step and strike should be coordinated. In this way, one will not lose the advantage.

Form-will, body-mind and mind-boxing are all Western translations of hsing-I. These suggest the intermingling of mind and body as the basic principle, but here the essence is usually misunderstood. The translation for hsing-I should be "heart and mind," for it is the heart that controls the emotions and fires the body's responses. Combining the heart and body with the will creates reactions that become natural and automatic, rather than stiff or contrived. As the mind begins to absorb the techniques, their usage becomes more instinctive. Often, if the heart is fearful, hesitation will result.

The most important point is learning to utilize the breath. Relaxing the body and mind produces movements that are natural and flowing. All action becomes natural and ultimately, the mind or will moves the body. The road is neither smooth nor easy, but with perseverance and an experienced teacher one can make significant progress.

Hsing-I is a defensive style where the opponent is allowed to make the first move and is then drawn into the counterattack. However, this is combined with our streetfighting theories, which allow for attacking first in a multiple-attacker situation. The defensive theory gives birth to the theory of "touch-go-kiss" and "true-not-true" or changing a technique as the opponent moves. As the opponent attacks, one must take the first step to deflect or "touch" the strike away. At the same time you "go" or penetrate deeply into the opponent, close enough to "kiss" or defeat him, by using any of the seven stars techniques. This requires speed and delicate sensitivity to incoming force and above all, regular practice.

Hsing-I is a soft style, which means that receiving and manipulating the opponent is just as important as striking. The opponent's force is used against him and allows one to pull him into a vortex of whirling destruction. Every vital spot is a target in one furious barrage. The circle is completed and maximum power is transferred.

Because of the inherent danger in this system, to defeat someone is not the most important aspect. It is balancing a respect for all life with respect for your own.

A shock punch, as the name implies, is a method of punching which delivers a great shock to the opponent. The shock is generated by the recoiling motion of your body at the same moment the punch connects with the opponent.

Hsing-I is a style that relies on soft, natural movements. Even though softness is essential to properly executing the techniques, a well-conditioned body that can withstand the punishment of an opponent is a necessary requirement. Thus, hsing-I movements will strengthen the body inside and out. Knowledge of technique is not enough, for even the best technician can be taken by surprise.

The Essence of Hsing-I

There are three principles of hsing-I: refine "ching," or seminar essence, to chi; refine chi to "shin," or spiritual essence; refine "shin" back into emptiness, or prenatal awareness. The three major steps are: modify bones; modify muscles; modify the spinal cord. The three ways to practice hsing-I are: visible strength; invisible strength; refined inner strength.

These principles will help you transform your mind and body to its prenatal state. The Chinese believe that a child's mind is like a blank tape. After years of problems and troubles, the slate must be wiped clean. This is the objective of hsing-I. It is common knowledge that most children heal faster and are generally more fit and flexible. Returning to this condition will make you physically and mentally healthy and help prolong your life.

Hsing-I involes two levels of study. The first consists of understanding the way of power, naturally cultivating the chi and defeating an opponent in no sign. The second level consists of learning how to dissolve power, learning how to change the marrow in the body, and achieving a state of spiritual emptiness.

Hsing-I, along with paqua and tai chi, comprise the wu tang system or internal style as opposed to external Shaolin styles.

The 12 animals of hsing-I are: dragon, tiger, monkey, horse, tortoise, cock, phoenix, sparrow hawk, swallow, snake, eagle and bear. Their spiritual attributes, along with the five elements—metal, water, wood, fire, earth—comprise the hsing-I system. As an internal system, it is most concerned with chi cultivation. When chi is held in the lower abdomen or tan tien, the body will be harmonious and stable. When chi erupts from the tan tien, power is produced to work the forge of the will. The power is held within until used, then later regenerated. Every movement contains the theory of yin and yang or true not true. Every move must be creative and destructive and also combine long and short. It is important not to overemphasize the hard, explosive aspects of hsing-I; the study of both paqua and tai chi will insure against this.

Hsing-I's spirit lies in the tan tien or the lower stomach, approximately three fingers below the navel. All power and energy are conserved inside until needed, yet this power will never be fully tapped. One's attack or defense follows the heart and mind. The posture should be gentle and the power should be in harmony with hard and soft.

The Five Elements

Hsing-I is derived from the five elements and the characteristics and movements of animals. Following is a chart of the hsing-I movements and the intent of the chi.

Element	Style (Chuan)	Action of Chi
Metal	Splitting (P'chuan)	Like an ax falling
Water	Drilling (Tswan Chuan)	Like lightning
Wood	Crushing (Peng Chuan)	Like an arrow

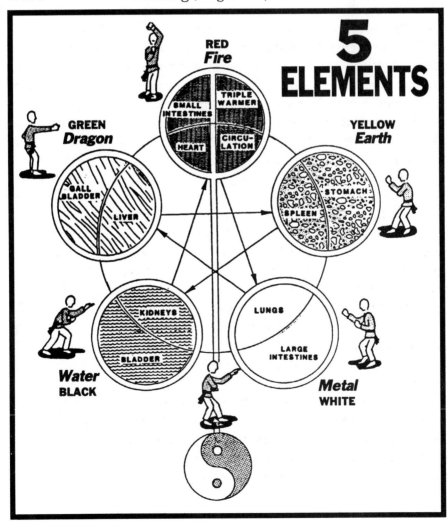

| Fire | Pounding *(Pao Chuan)* | Like firing a cannon |
| Earth | Crossing *(Heng Chuan)* | Round like a marble |

Alone, neither yin or yang can form life, nor can one exist without the other. In the body, every limb, bone and gesture is governed by yin and yang. When the two are harmonized, the body and its movements are strong. Without it, strength is scattered and the movements confused. For this reason yin and yang must be understood when practicing hsing-I. There is a relationship between hsing-I and life. Wu hsing means five elements or styles.

Creative and Destructive Cycle

The five elements of hsing-I were developed by observing and imitating the essential qualities of the natural forces. For instance, water always seeks its own leveL flowing downward and accumulating or sinking in. Fire, being less dense than water, rises. Wood can be made into a variety of shapes, either curved or straight. Metal can be forged, melted, refined and made pliable or unyielding. Earth is the source of nourishment and can generate all other elements. In hsing-I theory, the basis of the complementary relationships among the five elements is defined by the principles of mutual creation and mutual destruction.

According to the principle of mutual creation, metal creates water, water creates wood, wood creates fire, fire creates earth, and earth creates metal. In nature, the geologic and chemical forces at work within the earth serve to create metal. Metal itself becomes liquid as it melts when encountering sufficient heat. Water, combined with the nutrients of the earth, creates wood. Wood, in turn, creates fire, with the proper application of friction and heat. When wood is reduced to ashes it becomes a component of soil, thus creating earth.

The principle of mutual destruction holds that metal, in the form of tools, such as saws and axes, can destroy wood. The element of water overcomes fire. Wood can overcome earth by depleting the minerals and nutrients which make it fertile. Fire consumes wood and earth traps water in depressions or dams.

In the body, the internal organs are divided into yin and yang. Each organ is identified with one of the elements. The yin organs are: heart, spleen, lungs, kidney, liver. The yang organs are: small intestine, stomach, large intestine, bladder, gallbladder.

Correspondence Chart

The five elements theory constitutes the natural law governing the growth and decline of man. Chinese physicians began applying the theory of the five elements to the maintenance of health and the cure of illness thousands of years ago. The five elements theory stresses the interrelationships with the internal organs rather than their individual functioning, using the five elements principle of creative and destructive cycles.

The Chinese believe that a deficiency in one organ can affect another organ.

WOOD	FIRE	EARTH	METAL	WATER
Liver	Heart	Spleen	Lung	Kidney
Gallbladder	Sm. intestines	Stomach	Lg. intestines	Bladder
Eyes	Tongue	Mouth	Nose	Ear
Tendons	Arteries	Muscles	Skin	Bone
Nail	Complexion	Breast	Breath	Hair
Spring	Summer	Earth	Autumn	Winter
East	South	Center	West	North
Green	Red	Yellow	White	Black
Rank Smell	Burned	Fragrant	Frowzy	Rotten
Sour	Bitter	Sweet	Acrid	Salty
Breeze	Hot	Damp	Parch	Cold
Anger	Laugh	Think	Worry	Fear
Tear	Sweet	Mouth water	Nose running	Saliva
Crasp	Grief	Vomit	Cough	Tremble
Shout	Laugh	Sing	Weep	Groan
Chio	Chih	Kung	Shang	Yu
Wheat	Corn	Millet	Rice	Bean
Chicken	Lamb	Beef	Horse	Pork
Plum	Apricot	Date	Peach	Chestnut
Walk	Look	Sit	Lay down	Stand
Neck	Chest	Spine	Back	Waist
Mad	Joy	Afraid	Mournful	Fear

Western medicine, on the other hand, tends only to the diseased organ instead of the whole system of organs within the body.

If you have gallbladder or liver problems you will have tight tendons. The nails will also be affected and can show how long you have had this problem. The whites of the eyes will also have turned a shade of green and your neck will become very tight.

When you have a liver problem, you are afraid of the breeze, you easily become angry, tears will come often and your body will have a grasping or twitching action. Try not to live in the eastern part of the country. With a liver problem one shouldn't eat wheat, chicken or plums and don't walk too much. To help heal the gallbladder or liver, practice the wood form of hsing-I.

If you have a heart or small intestine problem, your tongue will be solidified or tight. Your chest will be tight and you will appear to be very happy (joy). Your face will turn red and your body odor will have a burning smell. You will have a fondness for bitter foods and you will be afraid of heat. You will laugh a lot and your body will sweat. Try not to live in the South because it is too hot and not beneficial for your heart. Don't eat corn, lamb or apricots. Don't stare too much. To help heal the heart or small intestine, practice the fire form of hsing-I.

If you have spleen or stomach problems, your lips will turn yellow. This problem also produces a fragrant smell in the body odor and you will enjoy eating sweets. The tightness will be around your spinal cord and you will always be afraid. If you have sickness in the spleen your joints will be damp and your underarms will be wet at all times. Try not to live in the middle of the country. You will also vomit a lot. You should not eat millet, beef or dates, and don't sit too long in one spot. To help heal the spleen or stomach, practice the earth form of hsing-I.

If you have lung or large intestine problems your nose will usually bother you and your skin will usually turn white. You will have a running nose and cough a lot. Try to avoid living in the West because it's not beneficial to your lungs. Don't eat rice, horse meat or peaches. Your back will be very tight and don't lay down too often. You might also feel mournful. To help heal the lungs or large intestine, practice the metal form of hsing-I.

If you have kidney or bladder problems, remember that these organs are associated with your urine and the water will go to your ears. This will make the inner eardrum wet, so it will be hard to hear and you will begin having ear problems. Try to avoid living in the North because it is cold and wet. You should not eat beans, pork or chestnuts. If you stand too long your body will feel uncomfortable and your bones and waist will hurt. You might also feel fearful most of the time. To help heal the kidney or bladder, practice the water form of hsing-I.

Hsing-I Originates Back to Nature

Hsing-I is like the beginning of life. You start from emptiness, then receive the warmth of the mother, then spirit or chi, then vigor; this starts a child forming, which in turn starts movement. When you have movement you know you have life. This is the natural process of development. But when one starts practicing kung-fu, one starts in the reverse of nature. First, you have the hard forms like karate or Shaolin kung-fu. The second step is the soft forms such as hsing-I, paqua and tai chi. The final step is emptiness or meditation.

Hsing-I consists of the five elements: metal, water, wood, fire and earth. Each element has a corresponding fighting technique in which one can defeat the other. Thus, a star configuration is formed like the one shown here.

By following the arrows and applying a little logic, one can see that metal defeats wood, as an ax bites into a tree trunk, eventually felling the mighty oak. Wood will defeat earth, as wood in the form of trees grow and cover our mother Earth. Earth will then conquer water, as earth muddies the water and subsequently turns water into earth. Water will destroy fire because this element can overcome the fiercest conflagration. Finally, fire will overcome metal as the heat of the blacksmith's forge melts iron. The creative and destructive natures of the five elements work toward a common end. The tao of the creative is used in building up body fitness, increasing power, strength and energy. The tao of the destructive is used in fighting and self-defense. Putting together the two natures of the five elements will teach one how to change his reaction to an attack when facing an opponent.

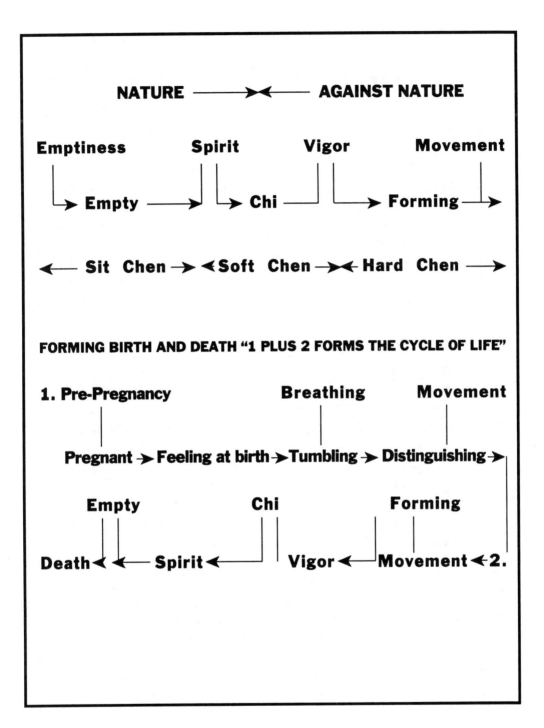

NATURE ——————►◄—————— **AGAINST NATURE**

Emptiness   **Spirit**   **Vigor**   **Movement**

└──► **Empty** ————► └► **Chi** ———— └──► **Forming** ——►

◄——— **Sit   Chen** ——► ◄**Soft   Chen** ——►◄ **Hard   Chen** ——►

FORMING BIRTH AND DEATH "1 PLUS 2 FORMS THE CYCLE OF LIFE"

1. Pre-Pregnancy   **Breathing**   **Movement**

Pregnant ➤ **Feeling at birth** ➤ **Tumbling** ➤ **Distinguishing** ➤

Empty   **Chi**   **Forming**

Death ◄ ◄——— **Spirit** ◄——— **Vigor** ◄——**Movement** ◄ **2.**

Master's Poem

The Chinese masters would sometimes write the actions of their art into a poem. The following is a translation of a poem given to me by Hsu Hung-Chi.

Metal (*Pi Chuan*)

From underneath the chin, the two closely spaced fists thrust forward to the level of the eyebrows. The right hand is forward, followed by the left. As the arms cross, the left hand goes forward. The heart unites, and the chi descends to the tan tien as the body begins to move. Place the left foot forward as the hands separate. The hu kou "tiger mouth" opens with all the fingers held in a crescent. The front hand pushes to a point between the eyebrows and the heart. The rear hand stays below the level of the armpit. Hands, nose and feet form the three-point set. In pi chuan, keep the little fingers turned up as the hands thrust upward. Sink the feet and hands together. The tongue is kept at the roof of the mouth. In advancing and changing styles, the rear palm sinks downward.

Water (*Tsuan Chuan*)

The forehand hand "yin palm" presses down. The rear hand "yang fist" thrusts up. The fist strikes to the level of the eyebrows. Elbows embrace the heart as the rear foot moves. Gaze at the forward hand. Stop the movement of hands and feet. Styles change like flowing water. Front foot steps first, back foot follows. Rear hand faces down, the elbows sink. Step by step, keep the three-point set. Forward hand strikes the nose. Your little finger turns upward. Protect the heart with the elbows. Tsuan chuan strikes the nose upon advancing. Forward hand presses down, then turns up as you step forward.

Wood (*Peng Chuan*)

Peng chuan starts with the three-point set. The hu yen point up as high as the heart. The front hand "yang fist" stays under the armpit. Step out with one foot, follow step with the other. Shaped like a "T," the feet are firm. Your body turns, while the eyes look straight. Keep the back straight when stepping. Toe out the foot when you move forward. Hands and feet move swiftly as one. One foot moves, the other follows naturally. Keep the tongue at the roof of the mouth. The arms are curved. Punch to the armpits when you advance, quick and firm. The rear foot follow steps.

Fire (*Pao Chuan*)

The elbows tightly embrace the body as you lift the foot. The "yang fist" must be firm. The chi falls to the tan tien as styles change. Keep the three-point set in place. Fists explode outward, up as high as the heart. The hu yen and elbows are kept downward. In pao chuan, the lead foot is on its toes, then steps out and drops as the fists thrust up. Step out diagonally with hands and feet coordinated. The rear foot follow steps.

Earth (*Heng Chuan*)

Forehand "yang fist," rear hand "yin." The rear hand is kept just below the elbow. Lift up the lead foot as the fists begin to move. With the body firm, the chi is settled. The tongue curls up and the air is exhaled. Half-turn the body while the hands and feet move. The rear hand twists, then thrusts upward. The fist, nose and feet are linked in one line. In heng chuan always keep the rear fist yin and the forward fist yang. Your elbows protect the heart. The left and right arms thrust out like bows. Hands and feet sink together. Keep the tongue at the roof of the mouth.

Five Element Forms

Metal (*Pi Chuan*)

Start with your feet together. The left foot is pointing straight forward, the right foot is at a 45-degree angle and the heels are touching. The right hand is resting on the left palm, facing upward with the tips of the thumbs touching. The eyes are looking straight ahead and the tongue is against the roof of the mouth. Breathe through the nose.

The hands are raised in an arc to the sides. Palms are up as you inhale. Upon reaching the highest point above the head, the hands come together with the thumbs and index fingers touching. The hands are then lowered together, down the center of the body, just below the navel, while exhaling. The knees bend slightly as the hands are lowered and the palms are facing downward. At all times one should be looking forward.

At this point, the hands turn upward while making a fist. Twist your body

a little to the left. The right fist then punches out and up to nose level and the left fist rests in the bend of the right elbow. The left fist follows the right arm upward, with the left hand opening as it reaches the right fist. The hand then strikes forward in a chopping motion (hands open), and you end the motion looking at your fingertips at nose level. The right hand drops in front of the stomach to protect the midsection. While stepping forward with the left foot, the weight is shifted to the right foot with the left foot lightly touching the ground. This is all executed in one movement.

With the left palm forward, squeeze both hands into fists and pull toward your navel. At the same time twist your body toward the center. The left fist punches out and up to nose level with the right fist resting in the bend of the left elbow. The right fist follows up to the left fist, then hits forward in a chopping motion. Once again you end the motion with hands open, looking at your fingertips at nose level. The left hand drops to the front of the stomach to protect the midsection. At the same time your hands are moving, you step forward with the right foot. The weight is shifted to the left foot, with the right foot lightly touching the ground. The left foot slides slightly forward to maintain balance. This is called a half-step and is very important in hsing-I. All this is executed in one movement. Repeat the same sequence on the left side.

Water (*Tsuan Chuan*)

Begin with the metal posture. The left hand is up and the right hand is down. The left hand twists counterclockwise with the palm up and the fingers come together as the left foot slides forward carrying the majority of the weight. The toes point outward at a 45-degree angle. The left hand twists clockwise into a fist as the right hand and foot come forward in unison. The right hand is in a fist and punches out and up to nose level, while the left hand pulls down in front of the navel. The rising right fist follows a path inside that of the dropping left hand, which is in a fist (palm down). The right foot has stepped through to a forward position and the left follows in a sliding half-step as in metal. This is all executed in one movement. Repeat the same sequence on the right side.

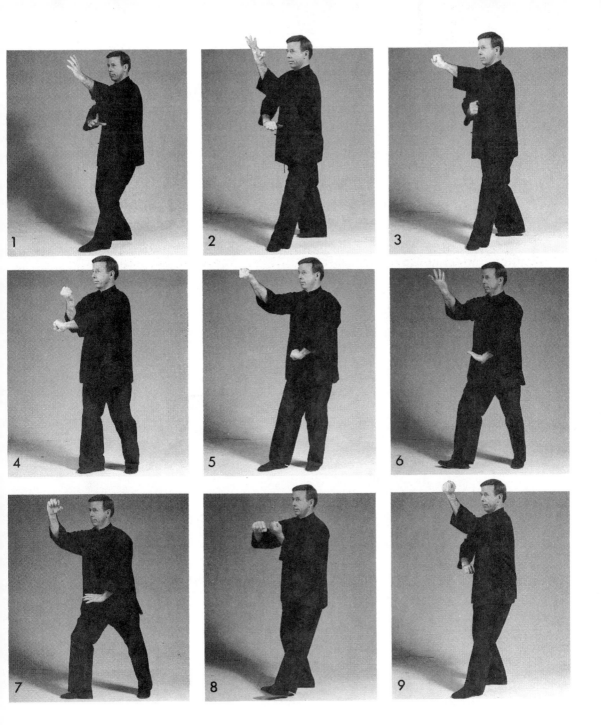

Wood (*Peng Chuan*)

Begin with the metal posture, with the left hand and foot forward. From this position the right hand forms a fist and is raised approximately to the solar plexus, then punches straight out. Simultaneously, the left hand goes to the side of the waist, curled in a fist. As the right hand punches, the right foot slides forward, alongside the left foot, about one inch behind the left toe, stopping with a shock punch.

Next, the left fist punches, coming out toward the center of the body in front of the solar plexus and brushing over the right arm, which is drawing back to the waist. In this step, the left foot moves out and the right foot follows with a sliding step alongside the left foot, about one inch behind the big toe. Repeat the same sequence on both sides.

Fire (*Pao Chuan*)

Begin with the metal posture. Step out at a 45-degree angle with your right foot. The left foot follows, while at the same time the hands close into fists which punch down alongside the stomach. Now you are facing inward in a cat stance with most of your weight on your right leg. The left foot is resting lightly alongside the right foot on the ball and toes. Step 45 degrees to the left with your left foot. At the same time, block upward with your left arm just above your eyes. The right fist punches to the midsection and the right foot follows with a half-step.

Next, step forward with your left foot and turn inward (clockwise). At the same time, the hands close into fists and punch downward alongside the stomach. Now you are facing inward in a cat stance with most of your weight on your left leg. The right foot is resting lightly on the ball and toes alongside the left foot. Step rightward in a 45-degree angle with your right foot. At the same time, block upward with your right arm just above your eyes as the left fist punches to the midsection. The left foot follows with a half-step. Repeat the same sequence on both sides.

Earth (*Heng Chuan*)

Begin with the metal posture. The footwork of earth is the same as the footwork in fire. Begin stepping 45 degrees to the right into a cat stance. The right foot is flat, the left foot is on its toes. Now step out left as your right fist circles clockwise and punches outward, in line with your nose, palm up. As you punch, the right fist rubs the underside of the left forearm, beginning contact at the left elbow. As the right fist strikes outward at nose level, the left fist twists palm down, just in front of the navel. The right foot follows the left in a half-step.

Next, step forward with your left foot and turn inward (clockwise), leaving the right fist in the same position. Now you are facing inward in a cat stance with most of your weight on your left leg, the right foot is resting lightly on the ball and toes alongside the left foot. Step out to a 45-degree angle with your right foot as the left follows in a half-step. Simultaneously, the left fist rubs the underside of the right forearm beginning contact at the elbow and strikes outward about nose level. As the right fist drops to the navel it twists to face palm down. Repeat the same sequence on both sides.

Metal (*Pi Chuan*) Fighting

Start in your hsing-I stance. The man on the right, B, kicks toward A. A blocks B's kick using both hands, then half-steps inward while simultaneously blocking B's punch while hitting him at the same time in the head.

Water (*Tsuan Chuan*) Fighting

Start in your hsing-I stance. The man on the left B, punches toward the face of A. A steps to the side and blocks the punch of B, while grabbing the punch and simultaneously hitting B's face.

Wood (*Peng Chuan*) Fighting

Stand in your hsing-I stance. The man on the left, B, uppercuts A's stomach. A uses wood punch and blocks B's uppercut while simultaniously hitting B in the ribs Then A, quickly using the wood punch, hits B's solar plexus.

Fire (*Pao Chuan*) Fighting

   Stand in your hsing-I stance. The man on the left, B, throws a roundhouse to A's face. A using Fire, blocks B's punch while simultaneously hits him in the solar plexus. B reacts and throws another punch toward A. A quickly counters using Fire again and defeats him.

Earth (*Heng Chuan*) Fighting

Stand in your hsing-I stance. The man on the left, B, throws his left punch to A's face. A steps to the side then using earth, blocks B's punch while simultaneously hitting B in the face. A can also break or dislocate B's arm at the same time he is hitting B with his shoulder.

Linking the Five Forms

After you have mastered these five forms individually, you can begin to put them into a form called wu hsing or five animal chain.

Start with your feet together, the left foot pointing straight forward, the right foot at a 45-degree angle. The heels are touching. The right hand is on the left palm, facing upward with the tips of the thumbs touching. The eyes are straight ahead. While breathing through the nose, the tongue is against the

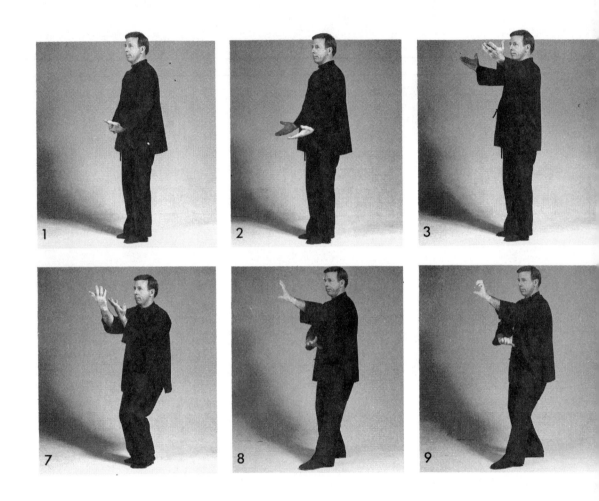

palate of the mouth. The hands are raised in an arc to the sides, palms up as you inhale. Upon reaching the highest point above the head, the hands come together with the thumbs and index fingers touching. The hands are lowered, the palms are facing downward. Look forward at all times. At this point, the hands turn upward while making a fist. Twist your body a little to the left. Then the right fist punches out and up to nose level. The left fist rests in the bend of the right elbow. Next, it follows the right arm upward. The left hand

Continued

opens as it reaches the right fist, then goes forward in a chopping motion with the hands open. You are now looking at your fingertips at nose level while the right hand drops a little in front of the stomach to protect the midsection. While stepping forward with the left foot, the weight is shifted to the right foot, with the left foot lightly touching the ground. This is all executed as one movement.

Now squeeze your fists, pulling them toward your stomach, palms down. At this point the fists turn upward, while twisting the body a little to the left.

Then, the left fist punches out and up to nose level. The right fist rests in the bend of the left elbow. The right fist follows the left arm upward and the right hand opens as it reaches the left fist. Then it goes forward in a chopping motion with the hands open as you are looking at your fingertips, which are at nose level. The left hand drops a little in front of the stomach. Step forward with the right foot at the same time. Shift the weight to the left foot while the right foot lightly touches the ground. This is all executed as one movement.

Now that you are in the metal posture, the right hand is up and the left hand is down. The right hand twists clockwise with the palm up and the fingers together as the right foot slides forward carrying the majority of the weight. The toes point outward at a 45-degree angle. The right hand twists counter-clockwise and makes a fist, as the left hand and foot come forward in unison. The left hand is in a fist and punches out and up to nose level, while the right hand pulls down in front of the navel. The rising left fist follows a path inside that of the dropping right hand, which is in a fist, palms down. The left foot has stepped through to a forward position and the right follows in a sliding half-step as in metal. This is all executed as one movement.

With the left fist punching forward, the left foot takes a half-step forward. At the same time, the right fist punches at about solar plexus level outward. The right foot slides forward alongside the left foot about an inch behind the left toe, stopping with a shock punch. Now, the left foot takes a half-step forward, while at the same time the left fist punches outward at about solar plexus level. The right foot slides forward alongside the left foot about an inch behind the left toe, stopping with the shock punch.

With the left fist forward, step at a 45-degree angle with the right foot. The left foot simultaneously follows. The hands close into fists and hit downward alongside the stomach. Now you are facing inward, in a cat stance, with most of your weight on your right leg. The left foot rests lightly on the ball and toes alongside your right foot. Step left to a 45-degree angle with your left foot and at the same time block upward with your left arm just above your eyes. Simultaneously the right fist punches to the midsection. The right foot follows with a half-step.

Turn your body inward 45 degrees. The left arm blocks down and the right fist punches upward. You are now in a cat stance with most of your weight on your left leg. Begin stepping at a 45-degree angle with your right foot. The left foot follows, while at the same time, the right fist is hitting upward at about nose level. Simultaneously, the left fist rubs the underside of the right forearm, beginning contact at the elbow, and strikes outward about nose level. As the right fist drops to the navel it twists palm downward. Bring the left arm downward, while the right fist simultaneously goes to the elbow of the left arm. The right foot slides a little ahead of the left foot and most of the weight is now on the left foot. The left fist is now at the elbow of the right arm. Now step forward with the left foot, while the left fist follows the right arm upward and the left hand opens as it reaches the right fist. Then strike forward in a chopping motion with the hand open. You are looking at your fingertips at nose level while the left hand drops in front of the stomach in the metal stance.

The Turn

Turn toward the right, squeeze both hands into a fist and hit your stomach. The knees are touching and the toes are pointing inward. The right fist hits upward to the side and the left fist follows the right arm, ending up in the metal stance. Now follow the same steps backward.

Breathing Application for the Five Elements

By practicing the five elements every day, one learns to condition the mind and body and also improve his fighting ability. The inner organs of the body will be conditioned because of proper breathing and posture and the chi will strengthen the different organs.

Metal   Start in your pi chuan stance. Stare at your index finger and breathe slowly from your lower stomach. Inhale and exhale three-to-five times thinking only of your lungs and filling them with chi. Then continue doing the metal form slowly, breathing on both sides right and left.

Water   Start in your pi chuan stance. Make the first move of the water form. Stare at the index finger and concentrate on your kidneys. Inhale and exhale, three-to-five times slowly, thinking only of filling your kidneys with chi.

Wood   Start in your pi chuan stance. Make the first move of the wood form. Stare at the fist and concentrate on your liver. Inhale and exhale slowly, three-to-five times, thinking only of filling your liver with chi.

Fire   Start in your pi chuan stance. Make the first move of the fire form. Stare at the fist and concentrate on your heart. Inhale and exhale slowly, three-to-five times, thinking only of filling your heart heart with chi.

Earth   Start in your pi chuan stance. Make the first move of the earth form. Stare at the fist and concentrate on your spleen and stomach. Inhale and exhale slowly, three-to-five times, thinking only of filling the spleen with chi.

Continue doing each form slowly, over and over again, at least 20 minutes per day for every organ you wish to strengthen. Breathe slowly through your lower abdomen and concentrate on a particular organ. The best time is early in the morning or late in the evening. Do not eat or drink anything one hour before or after doing the exercise. Take a bath or shower before doing these exercises, not afterward.

Five Element Fighting

This brings us back to the beginning. The continuing cycle is the basis of a form called the wu hsing, or two-man fighting set.

In the following pictures, two men are competing with each other. The man on the right side is A, while the man on the left side is B. They begin by standing opposite each other in the hsing-I stance. First, B moves forward with his left foot and punches with his right fist, using the wood punch. Then, A draws backward and blocks the punch. B moves ahead with his left foot while punching with his left fist against the face of A, using a wood punch. During this time, A steps to the side and turns his left fist upward before striking with his right hand to B's face. This is called the metal defeating the wood. During this time, B turns his left wrist upward with speed and force so that A's hand is compelled to go with it, leaving his middle part unprotected. This gives B a chance to punch with his right fist against A's belly. This is called fire defeating metal. At that moment, A steps back to the front while drawing down his left hand, grasping B by the wrist. A then punches B in the neck or chin. This is called water defeating fire. B then punches his left hand to the front with force against A's right arm, then punches with his right fist to A's face. This shows that earth conquers water. A withdraws his right hand and simultaneously punches with his left hand directly against B's stomach. This shows that wood can conquer earth. After this form is completed it is continued without stopping, over and over again.

Continued

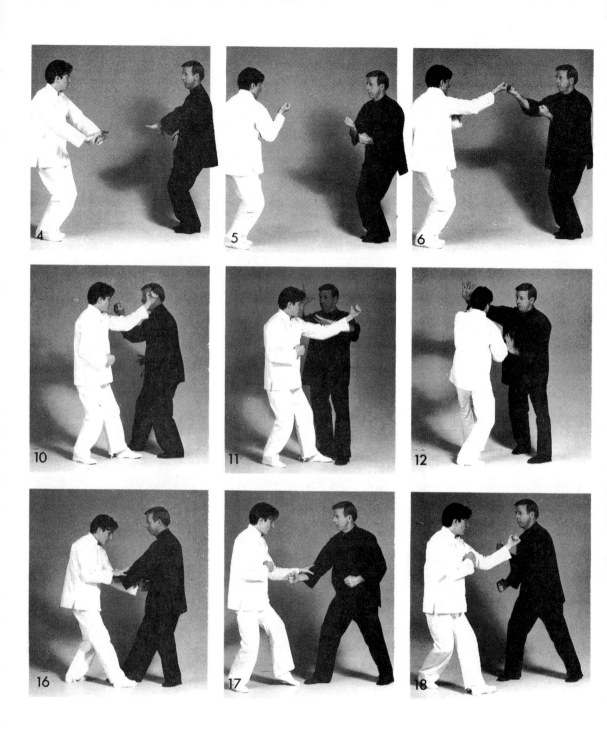

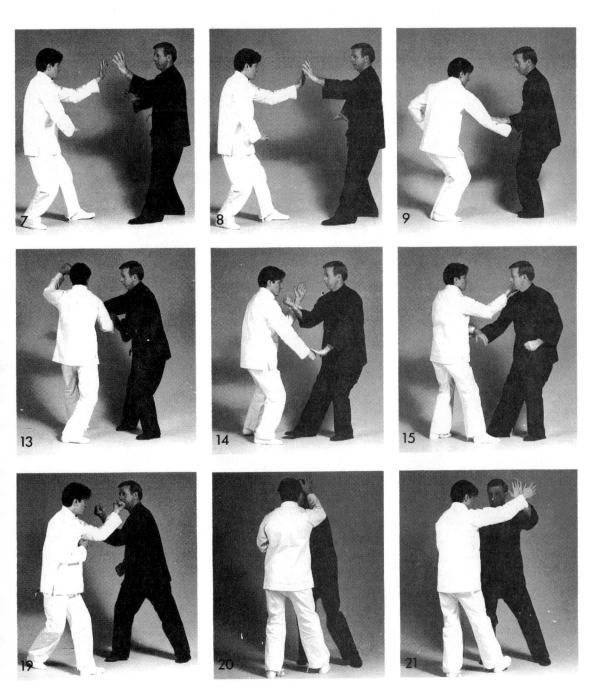

Continued

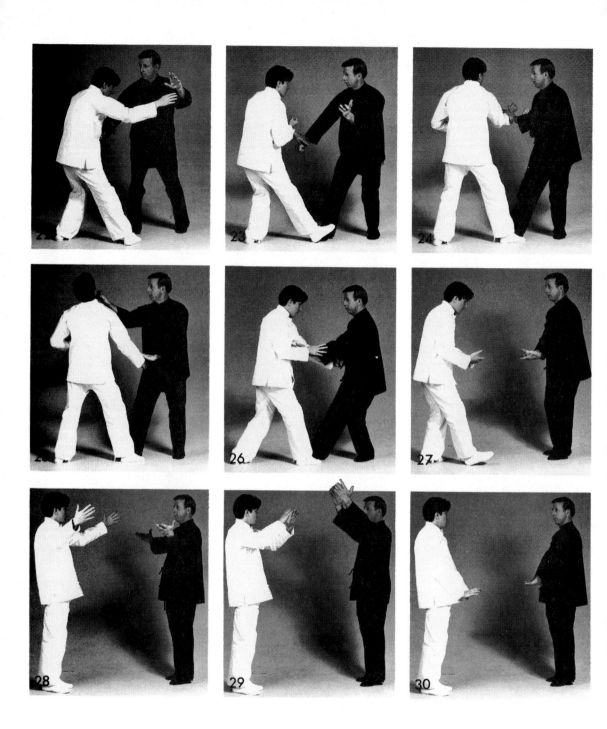

Common Mistakes

To truly learn how to capture the devastating power of hsing-I you must avoid making some common mistakes. However, it is inevitable that in learning something new the beginner will have problems. This is only natural. It is why we all must have qualified teachers who can correct these errors for us. This section demonstrates some of the most common mistakes made by many hsing-I students. It will help you overcome these mistakes and learn how to use the power of the elements, which is central to the true art of hsing-I.

Every movement and every position of the body has a meaning. These movements have been preserved over time for special purposes. Whether or not the student can comprehend this depends on the quality of his instruction and the length of time he has studied. To modify an art, which has been in existence for over a 1,000 years, it takes a man with great skill who, in most cases, is assuming that by modifying a position or movement he is improving it. In reality, he is improving it only for himself. Generally speaking, attempts to modify an ancient art such as hsing-I should not be made, since the essential elements may be lost in the process. It should be kept as pure and as close to its origins as possible.

What follows are a few of the most serious mistakes made concerning the basic principles. An important part of hsing-I is to hold your balance. If you can keep your balance when throwing your opponent, you can emerge victorious. Stay rooted, keeping your back straight.

Incorrect: Don't ever overextend your body.

Correct: Keep your back straight and your feet rooted.

Incorrect. Don't overextend the elbow past the knee when pushing.

Correct: In pushing you should always have your back straight, elbows down, and feet rooted.

Incorrect: You have no power when you bend forward at the waist.

Correct: Sink your weight and keep your back straight. This will send any opponent down with tremendous force.

Incorrect: With the elbow kept up there is a loss of power and the ribs are exposed.

Correct: Keep the elbow down for more devastating power in your punch.

Incorrect: With the supporting leg straight and the knee locked there won't be as much power in your kick.

Correct: With the supporting leg bent and rooted, you have more driving power in your kick.

Incorrect: When punching, the hand is not turned and the tendons are loose, so you won't have as much power.

Correct: If the wrist is twisted like a rope you will have much more shocking power in your punch.

The Twelve Animals

English Word	Chinese Word
Dragon	Lung
Tiger	Hu
Monkey	Hou
Horse	Ma
Turtle	Tow
Chicken	Gi
Phoenix	Tai
Sparrow-Hawk	Yao
Swallow	Yen
Snake	Sner
Eagle/Bear	Ing Hsing
Fighting Chicken	Dou Gi

Please Note:
Due to the complexity of the forms shown,
I am only able to show, with photographs,
small segments of each form.

Dragon

Dragon

The dragon heads the list of the 12 animals. This form is used mainly to train for the rising and falling of the body, the bending and stretching of the arms, and the jumping and changing of kicks.

Form

Open with the hsing-I stance. Block across the midsection, rotating the forearm. Simultaneously, grab with the right hand and kick with the instep of the right foot, while you drop to the ground. The weight is on the rear leg and the right leg is extended forward. The right fist is at the right hip and the left hand is forward by the extended right foot. Spring up like an uncoiling dragon and split the hands as in metal. Then, while in the air, kick both feet outward in a scissoring motion, landing with the left leg forward. The left fist is at the hip and the right hand is held forward near the extended foot. Spring upward

again, with the hands split as in metal. Repeat the scissoring kick, landing this time with the right leg forward, the right fist at the hip and the left hand forward by the extended foot.

Repeat the dragon spring. Notice the right foot is forward as you now begin to stand up and punch the right fist with the feet together. Now, punch again and step with the left foot forward in an open stance. Block across the midsection, rotating the forearm, simultaneously grabbing with the left hand and kicking with the instep of the left foot, while dropping to the ground. The weight is on the rear leg and the left leg is extended. Spring up as before, landing with the right leg forward. Step up and in and punch with the right fist in a closed stance. Follow with an open left stance, punching twice. Then turn and repeat the whole sequence again but go back in the opposite direction.

3

4

7

Fighting

Two men face each other. The man on the left, B, punches with the right fist to the midsection of A. A, with his right arm moving in a circling motion, blocks and grabs the opponent's arm, while using his right foot to kick the opponent in the knee. Then he steps on B's knee to take him down and simultaneously strike the head.

Tiger

Tiger

The tiger is considered to be the king of all animals. It represents a kind of strength coming from the tan tien. The tiger is characterized by its fierce external appearance combined with a great internal softness. A very famous movement of the tiger is the double-handed push. The hands and fingers represent the jaws and teeth of the tiger as he is about to attack. The ancient Chinese observed the tiger's behavior and turned it into a defensive movement, whereby the attacker is pushed out of range or destroyed depending on the power one uses. Practicing this form can give one enormous power.

Form

Start with the hsing-I stance. Step to the right at a 45-degree angle with the right foot and go into a cat stance. At the same time squeeze the hands into a

fist and bring them to your waist. Then, without stopping, step to a 45-degree angle inward. The left foot steps forward in a left stance. At the same time hit outward with your hands about kidney level. Next, take one step forward with the left foot, go into a cat stance and turn inward at a 45-degree angle. Squeeze the hands into a fist and bring them to the waist. Then, without stopping, hit outward opening your hands and hitting at the kidneys. The footwork is the same for both sides. Go upward.

Fighting

Two men face each other. The man on the left, B, punches with the right fist to the stomach of A. A blocks B with his right hand, turning him to the left. A, then pushes him away or destroys him internally by striking the kidneys.

Monkey

Monkey

The monkey is a lively, active and intelligent animal. It can climb and jump from tree to tree. He uses his agile hands and feet for many purposes. The direction and angle of its hand movements are different in character from those of other animals. If you frighten the monkey he will use a slapping defense on his aggressor. In fighting, don't underestimate the power of the slap. Such power can do great internal damage to an opponent's body.

Form

Start in a hsing-I stance. Turn your body around to the left, leaving your feet in position but making a "t." Punch up with the left fist about face level. Then,

with a slapping motion, slap downward at the same time while walking backward three steps. Then, half-step back into a cat stance and block with the left arm. Step and slap forward three times. Turn toward your back making a "t," hitting upward with the fist about face level. Slap and step forward three steps, then backward. Turn toward the left, follow the same process and then backward to finish the form.

Fighting

Two men face each other. The man on the left, B, punches with the right
fist to the solar plexus of A. A slaps both hands in a circular motion, blocking
B's hands. While A's hands are still moving, he slaps to the face or heart or
blocks B's hands simultaneously kicking to the groin. Again don't underestimate the power of the slap. It can be very devastating.

Horse

Horse

The horse is a fast and powerful animal. While engaged in fighting, a horse will rear on its hind legs and strike with its front hooves. In the application of this form, the movement of the upper and lower parts of the body must be in proper balance. This will show the strong and powerful characteristics of this style.

Form

Open with the hsing-I stance. Form both hands into fists. Bring them down about waist level. Simultaneously, step to the right side with the right foot.

Strike upward with both fists at the same time, then strike in a downward motion. Then, step forward with the left foot. Repeat this movement left to right.

Fighting

Two men face each other. The man on the left, B, punches with the left fist to the face of A. A uses both arms in a circling block upward and outward, then steps in to hit B in the face or chest.

Tortoise

Tortoise

The tortoise is a powerful animal, especially in the water. When training in this style it is particularly important to coordinate the movement of the upper and lower parts of the body. The whole body is lively and resilient, with the emphasis placed on the turning of the waist, which constitutes the center of movement for the body.

Form

Start in a hsing-I stance. Step and turn 90 degrees to the left with the left foot in a circular motion followed by the right foot. Simultaneously rotate the left hand palm up and arm stretched out. The nose is aligned with the forefinger. At the same time, the right hand blocks palm down at the level of the navel.

The left foot is straight forward and the right foot is at the left instep approximately one-quarter inch off the ground. The right foot sweeps outward in a semicircular arc and the body follows in a 180-degree forward turn. The right hand moves as the body turns, stretching outward with the palm rotating up. The left hand moves downward to an inside position at the waist. Repeat this sequence to the end of your practice space. Turn while in the left position and step backward with the left foot, repeating the above sequence, only now going backward.

Fighting

Two men face each other. The man on the left, B, punches with the left fist to the face of A. A simultaneously moves one step to the side and blocks with his right arm. He simultaneously hits B with his left hand.

Cock

Cock

The form has a combined series of movements imitating the features of the cock. By advancing and retreating and using the various hand and foot movements, along with specific body changes, it brings about a state of confusion in one's opponent. The cock sometimes fights on one leg and in the form we imitate this movement. He also uses his wings, beak and claws. The beak pecks, grabs or pulls and the wings flap around while the claws stamp and kick.

Form

Start with your feet together and hands to the side. Move the hands in a circular block while dropping downward to protect the knees. Quickly spring up, while simultaneously raising the hand above the head. Then, drop the

hands down in the metal form with the left foot forward. Step forward with left foot, at the same time poking forward with the right hand. Step again with the left foot and this time hit with the left chicken fist. Repeat this twice. Then, with the left foot forward, punch with the right fist and circle block with both hands. Then block, first with the right arm, then with the left arm, while turning and simultaneously kicking with the instep of the left foot. This movement is done while slapping upward and dropping downward. Spring up quickly and flap the arm outward and into the metal form. Block with the left arm in a circular block, then punch. Skip the feet with the left foot forward. Block with the right arm and let the left arm slap upward and then drop. Spring up quickly and flap the arms outward and into a metal stance. Finish the form.

Fighting

Two people face each other. The man on the left, B, kicks at the knees of A. A drops and blocks B with a circular block. B then punches at A's face. A springs up and blocks B's punch. A then hits B in the throat using his fingers.

Phoenix

Phoenix

In Chinese mythology, the Phoenix, a sign a of good luck, is represented by two birds, one male and one female. Entwined together they die engulfed in flames. They rise from their ashes, reborn, flapping their mighty wings skyward. When the Phoenix flaps its wings this emphasizes its form and intention. The form is the flapping motion and the intention is to fly. We imitate this movement with our arms and fists.

Form
'Start in a hsing-I stance. Step to the right in a 45-degree angle, simultaneously circling your hands around your head. When your hands are at your

waist level you should be in a cat stance. Turn 45 degrees and face inward. Step inward and at the same time hit upward about solar plexus level. Now on the other side, step while circling your hands above you head. When your hands are at your waist level you should be in a cat stance; turn and face inward. Step to a 45-degree angle and at the same time hit upward about solar plexus level. Now, you are on the other side. Do this movement three times. Turn and do the same form backward.

Fighting

Two people face each other. The man on the left, B, chokes the man on the right, A. A circles his hands upward, breaks the chokehold and quickly hits B in the ribs or stomach.

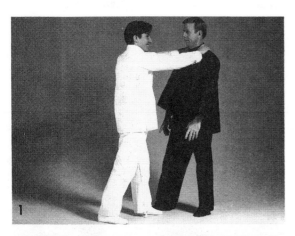 

3

4

Sparrow-Hawk

Sparrow-Hawk

The sparrow-hawk looks similar to the eagle but is much smaller. He dives and twists to the ground with great speed to catch his prey. When doing the form you should imitate the open claws of the sparrow-hawk.

Form

Start in your hsing-I stance. Bring the left hand down in a blocking motion about groin level, grab and raise your left hand to head level while stepping

forward with the right foot and punching with the right hand. Block the right hand down with a claw hand, grab, then follow through with the left hand under the right arm to grasp the throat. Turn and repeat these movements before returning to the starting position. Repeat this movement as many times as you wish.

Fighting

Two people face each other. The man on the left, B, throws a punch to the midsection. A blocks down while sinking his weight. While grabbing with the blocking hand he reaches under as he steps around and grabs the opponent by the throat. To complete the move he tears with his fingers like the beak of the sparrow-hawk, simultaneously breaking his arm with the shoulder.

Swallow

Swallow

The swallow is a small bird with long and powerful wings. It can fly at a high rate of speed and is light and swift. The swallow is not a bird which one normally thinks of as a fighter, but it can intimidate intruders by swooping down upon them. In doing this form, the student will learn that by moving the head and shoulders back just a little, he can evade a blow. If someone attacks his head, he can dive down and catch the opponent's leg, pulling it out from under him.

Form

Start in a hsing-I stance. Turn 90 degrees and block with an undercircular motion with both hands. Drop down in a swooping motion at a 90-degree angle

(in the starting direction). Spring up on your right leg with the right arm in the air and the left at the groin, then side kick with the left leg. Drop the leg and hit with the right hand at groin level. Twist the body backward while crossing the feet in a "t." Step forward and hit with the right hand at groin level and skip forward. Raise the left foot up about knee level. Drop down and hit with the left fist. Block with an undercircular motion with both hands. Drop in a swooping motion at a 90-degree angle. Repeat the same movements backward to finish the form.

3

4

Fighting

Two men face each other. The man on the left, B, kicks with the left foot to the face of A. A blocks quickly with both hands and steps forward, kicking the opponent's leg while simultaneously hitting him in the groin.

Snake

Snake

The snake is a legless reptile which moves quickly. Because of the snake's length it can attack animals with either its head or tail, or simultaneously with both the head and tail.

Form

Start off in a hsing-I stance. The left hand blocks upward above the head. Then close the hand into a fist as if grabbing, simultaneously sweeping the

right foot and stooping downward while striking downward with the right hand. Lunging upward with the right hand, strike at the groin level. Step forward with the right foot and raise the right hand above the head and close the fist as if grabbing. Simultaneously sweep the left foot and stoop while striking downward with the left hand. Lunge forward with the left hand and strike at the groin level. Repeat this move forward from side-to-side as many times as you want. Turn and do the same form in the opposite direction to finish the movement.

3

4

Fighting

Two men face each other. The man on the left, B, punches to the face of A. A blocks upward then circles his wrist grabbing B. A strikes with the edge of his hand to B, elbow rolling the arm over and forcing B to the floor. He can then step inward and hit B with his hand and body to destroy him.

Bear

Eagle/Bear

Mixing the eagle and bear styles feature the accuracy and boldness of an eagle in seizing its prey with the vigor and uprightness of the bear defending itself. In executing the form, you must keep the head, neck and body straight while standing upright like a bear. A person's arms must have the strength to overturn the arm of an attacker while the hands must drop like an eagle's claws.

Form

Start off with the hsing-I stance. Step to the right at a 45-degree angle, raising the left arm upward. Twist the hand and grasp, simultaneously striking

downward to the left with the open right hand, while stepping 45 degrees to the left. Step forward with the left foot, twist the hand and grasp, simultaneously striking downward to the right with the open left hand. Repeat this move as many times as you want, then turn and do the movements in the opposite direction to finish the form.

Fighting

Two men face each other. The man on the left, B, punches with the left fist to the face of A. A then steps to the side and grabs B's left hand with the eagle claw and uses his left hand to take B to the ground.

Fighting Chicken

Fighting Chicken

The fighting chicken has great physical power and courage. Some chickens even fight to the death. In this form, the hand and feet move like the chicken—fast and effective.

Form

Open with the pi chuan stance. The left foot leads and pivots outward while the left hand simultaneously lowers to waist level in an open palm, downward block. The right hand moves up to the centerline with the palm up, fist to nose level. This should be done in one smooth, coordinated movement. From this position, the left lead foot moves back with a stomp, one-half step, while the right rear foot comes forward into a cat stance, right foot forward. The hands then move to their respective sides of the head, slightly in front of the body. Strike downward with open palms as the right foot steps forward and the rear left foot half-steps forward with a stomp into place. The footwork is performed

with a one-two sequence, right foot steps, left foot half-steps. Repeat four times. Turn, with a rear arm block forward about nose level, with the fist palm up. The forward arm rides in front of your navel about wrist level. Pivot 180 degrees. The arms change position and the left arm executes the same block while the other arm wraps tightly along the body. From this crossed-arms position, both arms explode in opposite directions; one out and one back. Simultaneously, the rear leg kicks forward at knee level. Next, drop down to a kneeling cross-step stance with the left leg forward and the hands open fully and crossed in a high/low, left/right block. Quickly raise your hands and uncross, while the legs uncross with a stomp. The right foot is now forward and the left foot is to the rear. The left foot steps forward as you assume a left hand forward pi chuan stance. Repeat the sequence once more and then turn into the metal stance and close.

3

4

Fighting

   Two men face each other. The man on the left, B, strikes with the left fist to the face of A. A blocks with his right hand and simultaneously strikes upward to the face of B. B then strikes with the left hand and A responds by quickly blocking upward with the hands formed in a chicken's beak. A strikes B with the right hand on the collarbone and strikes the solar plexus with the left hand.

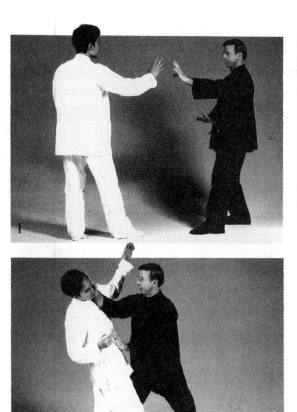

Push Hands

The two forces that govern the universe are known as yin and yang. These are also applied in push hands, which develops total body sensitivity. The practitioner develops a sense of touch which is transmitted through the skin. If you can get rid the body of all rigidity and force, then you will feel as if the body is there, yet not there. You will "listen" through your eyes by watching your partner's movements. Keeping contact with your partner's hands and

arms helps develop sensitivity. The sharpening of the sense of touch will lead to detecting your partner's moves.

The practitioner must be free from unnecessary tension by relaxing the legs, waist and arms. With practice, progress will come and the nervous system will be more alert and sensitive. You will learn to overcome the strong and hard by the gentle and soft way. Give up all resistance by becoming soft. Don't ever match force with your opponent; for the stronger will defeat the weaker.

Proper practice of the 12 animals yields the following

Dragon	Reduces fire in the body to a minimum.
Tiger	Purifies the breathing.
Monkey	Benefits mind and spirit. Promotes calming, pacifies the spirit.
Horse	Reduces anger in the mind; tonifies the heart.
Tortoise	Strengthens the "earth" element; tonifies the spleen and stomach.
Chicken	Benefits the tan tien; tonifies the liver.
Phoenix	Promotes circulation of the du and ren pulses; tonifies the kidneys.
Sparrow-Hawk	Fills the tan tien with chi; exercises the hypogastrium.
Swallow	Promotes suppleness in musculature: Improves mental coordination.
Snake	Rubs positive and negative chi; rubs yin and yang.
Eagle/Bear	Aids in circulation of breath.
Fighting Cock	Strengthens the "earth" element; tonifies the spleen and stomach.

The Healing Arts

Kung-fu encompasses far more than physical exercise and self-defense. Seldom does anyone realize that a complete kung-fu practitioner must be able to treat external as well as internal maladies; to heal as well as to kill. A kung-fu practitioner can diagnose and treat many maladies with herbs and other treatments. The Chinese have basically four methods of medicine: acupressure, acupuncture, moxibustion and herbology.

Acupuncture, which uses needles to stimulate or divert chi flow from one meridian to another, is an ancient Chinese system of medicine. The oldest written documents on acupuncture are found in Huang Ti's book on internal medicine. Even though acupuncture can be found in the histories of other countries, the Chinese have developed a complete method. The Chinese have classified the acupuncture points into 12 main and several minor meridians. The meridians on one side of the body correspond to those on the other side. The Chinese believe that chi activates all the processes of the body and that the meridians act as a passage for chi to flow to the diseased organ or site of the symptoms. Acupuncture is also used to keep the yin and yang in balance and in harmony within the body.

Acupressure, which uses the fingers as needles, includes the same meridians as acupuncture and may entail the knuckles, elbows or the heel of the hand. In acupressure massage heavy pressure is applied at an acupuncture point until the patient feels a relaxation in the muscle. As in acupuncture, acupressure's aim is to restore the natural balance of yin and yang to the body.

Moxibustion is a herbal preparation, like incense, that is used to heat an injured spot and to soak herbal smoke into the skin along the meridians. Based on heat, moxibustion is the nature of yang and very useful in treating diseases caused by the excess of yin. It can be applied by itself or affixed to the acupuncture points after the needle has been withdrawn. Studies have also shown that moxibustion increases the number of red corpuscles and hemogloblin within the body.

Herbology is widely used in today's system of Chinese health care. It has evolved over thousands of years through trial and error. Herbs can be taken in tea form or steeped in a alcoholic mixture for several months and drunk as a tonic. They can also be ingested in powder form or by chewing on the herb itself. Because of modern technology, raw herbs can now be purified and used in over-the-counter medicines.

Pressure Points

Every hsing-I student should acquire knowledge of pressure points or nerve points. Pressure points control is performed by hitting, kicking, rubbing or pinching at an opponent's vital points. Pressure control can cause acute pain to the opponent and short-term loss of retaliating capability. However, depending on the strike, death also can result.

There are many methods of controlling pressure points at various meridians along the body. However, action must be fast and strength must be applied appropriately and accurately. By knowing how chi circulates through the meridians and being well-versed in healing methods, an advanced student can reverse the healing knowledge and use it for destructive purposes.

The Lo-Shu

According to Chinese legend, the lo-shu is a diagram of change. It was discovered by Yu the Great on the back of a tortoise upon emerging from the Lo River.

During the liturgy, the Taoist's use the lo-shu as a basic floor plan for the rituals of the Chiao festival. It is drawn on the floor of the sacred ritual area.

It also is used in the practice of black magic. By dancing around the lo-shu, one is said to be able to summon the spirits. Lo-shu is also known as a magic square, because no matter which direction the numbers are added, the sum will always be 15. In using the lo-shu for hsing-I practice, place nine sticks as shown in the diagram. At first, make the distance between each stick a few feet apart. After your skill has increased, gradually decrease the distance until the sticks area shoulder-width apart. When moving between the sticks, make sure you are blocking or punching with each step. You should pretend that each stick is an opponent whom you are evading, blocking or striking.

The magic square or lo-shu resembles the following diagram:

Paqua

Paqua, or eight diagrams forms the basis of the I-Ching (Book of Changes) and is over 3,000 years old. The central theme of the book, as well as in its boxing, is based on the idea of continuous change. The eight diagrams represent the Chinese philosophy and the broken and unbroken lines are used to explain all natural phenomena

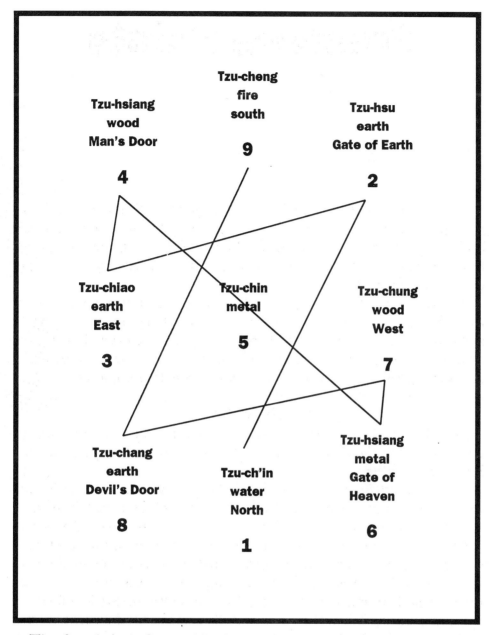

Tzu-cheng
fire
south
9

Tzu-hsiang
wood
Man's Door
4

Tzu-hsu
earth
Gate of Earth
2

Tzu-chiao
earth
East
3

Tzu-chin
metal
5

Tzu-chung
wood
West
7

Tzu-chang
earth
Devil's Door
8

Tzu-ch'in
water
North
1

Tzu-hsiang
metal
Gate of
Heaven
6

The foundation of paqua boxing is in the circling movement and its constant changes. By using a circular action one can impart great speed and power. The ultimate goal is to allow the body to move, act and react naturally.

The origins of paqua are unclear, but many believe the book originated before the era of Huang-Ti, the Yellow Emperor. Tung Hai-ch'uan (1798-1879), from the Hopeh province, was one of the great paqua masters. It is said that Tung learned his paqua from a Taoist in the mountains of Kianasu province.

After becoming famous, Tung Hai-ch'uan was challenged by Kuo Yun-Shen (Divine Crushing Hand), a hsing-I great. Kuo and Tung fought evenly for two days, but on the third day Tung took charge and easily defeated Kuo.

After the fight, they became lifelong friends. From then on, a student trained in hsing-I would also learn paqua and vice versa.

Shown below is the paqua chuan linage chart. As you can see many famous hsing-I masters have also studied paqua.

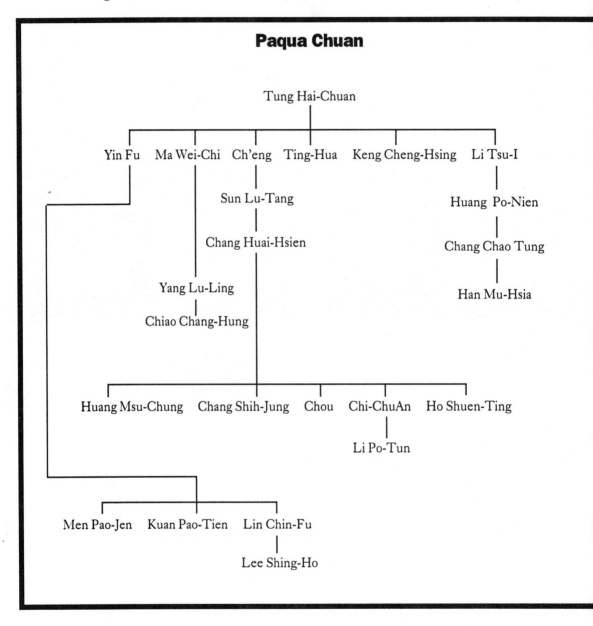

Paqua Chuan

Tung Hai-Chuan

Yin Fu Ma Wei-Chi Ch'eng Ting-Hua Keng Cheng-Hsing Li Tsu-I

Sun Lu-Tang

Huang Po-Nien

Chang Huai-Hsien

Chang Chao Tung

Yang Lu-Ling

Han Mu-Hsia

Chiao Chang-Hung

Huang Msu-Chung Chang Shih-Jung Chou Chi-ChuAn Ho Shuen-Ting

Li Po-Tun

Men Pao-Jen Kuan Pao-Tien Lin Chin-Fu

Lee Shing-Ho